SIEGFRIED W. RUDE[...]
rural setting of Silesia, th[...]
but now Poland. After the [...]
he was determined to finish his school years at a Steiner
Waldorf School, which he succeeded in doing. He
then trained in Special Education, first in Scotland and
then Switzerland. A group of four students returned to
England in 1951 to found a Home-School for 'maladjusted' children (as they were then referred to).
Siegfried has stayed the course throughout the Peredur Trust's 60
adventurous years to date. He is now the charity's President.

BY THE LIGHT OF THE LANTHORN

Working with People with Special Needs

A Cultural and Social Impulse in a Changing World

Siegfried W. Rudel

TEMPLE LODGE

Temple Lodge Publishing
Hillside House, The Square
Forest Row, RH18 5ES

www.templelodge.com

Published by Temple Lodge 2011

The publishers would like to thank the Committee for Steiner Special Education for their generous sponsorship of this book

A catalogue record for this book is available from the British Library

ISBN 978 1 906999 27 8

Cover by Andrew Morgan Design
Typeset by DP Photosetting, Neath, West Glamorgan
Printed and bound by Berforts, Herts.

In memoriam
Joan Rudel (née Hinchcliffe)
May her far-reaching aims live on in our good will

What is precious is never to forget . . .
Never to allow gradually the traffic to smother
With noise and fog the flowering of the spirit.

Stephen Spender (1909–95)

Lanthorn: an alternative spelling for "Lantern": Something enclosing a light, and protecting it from the wind, rain, etc.

Webster's Online Dictionary

Contents

Foreword, by Paul A. Clark, B.Sc.(Econ.), CQSW, ACWA   1

Introduction   4

THE FOUR FOUNDERS
1. Marguerite (Peggy) Jarvis (1915–2000)   9
2. Lore Richter (1923–2007)   13
3. Joan Hinchcliffe (later Rudel) (1915–2003)   18
4. Siegfried Rudel (b. 1928)   28

INTERLUDE   47

THEMES IN A PEREDUR NARRATIVE AND BEYOND
5. Special Schools—Yes or No?   57
6. The Environment—Obstacle or Opportunity?   68
7. Nutrition—Help or Hindrance?   81
8. 'For the Rhythm of Life is a Powerful Beat'   88
9. Music, Art and Crafts—Pleasantries or More Than That?   97
10. Work on the Land—Why and How?   107
11. Arne Klingborg, the Swedish Connection and the Lanthorn Press   122
12. The Steiner Committee for Special Needs—Can We Think Together?   134
13. Sustainability—How Far is it Possible?   139
14. What are the New Needs? *by Araminta Greaves*   142
15. *Quo Vadis*, Peredur? *by Paul A. Clark*   145
A Brief List of Events So Far   148

Who is Rudolf Steiner? A brief account of his life and work   151

Walk On A poem by Herman Hesse (1877–1962)   165

Further Reading   167

My profound thanks to Araminta Greaves and my wife Karin for their steady help and support, and to Paul Clark for suggesting the main title of the book.

'... The principles of Rudolf Steiner are those of religion expressed in a practical way ... The seeds sown by the Shaftesburys and the Nightingales and like minded people have grown into a great system of social welfare of which we are entitled to be proud. But any system, however enlightened, must be challenged by fresh awareness of new and changing needs. In this the voluntary trusts like Peredur have an important place.'

Professor Fulton, Vice Chancellor of Brighton University, May 1964

Foreword

As one of those difficult and contrary readers who tends to ignore foreword or preface pages when I take up a book, I even afford the contents list no more than a cursory glance before heading straight for Chapter 1.

Only after covering enough of the tome to determine that I wish to read further and learn more might I sheepishly return to any foreword. If you are one who shares this unforgivable habit, I can only assume that you have now reached the stage where your interest has been sufficiently aroused for you to be seeking wider knowledge about these exceptional people who came together through a shared inspiration. They were determined to help and motivate so many lost, bewildered, disregarded and even abandoned children and young people whose only 'crime' might be their failure to communicate with the wider world.

Whichever reason or reading method brings you to these few paragraphs, may I welcome you to Siegfried Rudel's characteristically modest summary of this special work and remarkable achievements—of victories for compassion and common sense, often won against formidable and overwhelming odds.

I was among the ranks of such formidable adversaries when my duties took me to my first meeting with Joan and Siegfried in 1990. Employed by the County Social Services department for some 20 years, I had recently received an unsought and far from welcome promotion to Head of the Inspection Unit.

Following visits to the Peredur establishments, inspectors accountable to me submitted their recommendations that Basill Manor and Trebullom should be served with notices to comply with various regulations or face closure.

There was no doubt that some changes would need to be phased in to comply with the Registered Homes Act, but Peredur had been caring for disadvantaged and differently-abled young people effectively and successfully for over 40 years by that time, so I decided that I should arrange a personal visit to these unusual people who had so disturbed my officers. My aim was to investigate the problem and, if possible, negotiate some less draconian way forward.

However, by then Joan and Siegfried had contacted the Trust's solicitor, one of the senior partners in an internationally famous legal firm. He had firmly advised them against seeing me or even speaking to me until my local authority had submitted in writing their reasons for, and intentions behind my visit.

I telephoned Joan to say that I had only wanted an informal meeting and chat! However, she said she would refer back to her solicitor and I would simply have to wait. Although I did have a statutory right to turn up and insist on seeing them, I chose to exercise my discretion and wait a while.

None of the inspection reports had indicated that residents were considered to be at risk in any way. The main criticisms centred on lack of written policies and procedures—shared rooms, no television, no 'evidence' of choice in the residents' activities, in summary, to paraphrase: 'Too regulated, too like a school, too little choice'.

Accepting then that I would be waiting a while in the hope of an eventual amicable discussion, I decided to prepare for this by learning what I could about this 'Rudolf Steiner'—reference to whom appeared on the Peredur Trust letterhead. This, not surprisingly, led me to read a synopsis or two about something called 'anthroposophy' (a word which, incidentally, some 20 years on, I finally feel competent to pronounce).

By the time the delayed meeting took place, I had been advised that I would be encountering members of a 'cult' which advocated behavioural therapy for its clients and residents. 'Arrive late for your meal and next time you would have only bread and water; arrive late a second time that same week and you will find only pebbles on your plate.' 'Crops could only be planted by the light of the moon and according to the movement of planets—then only harvested according to a Scandinavian Calendar.' 'Eurythmy was practised as a form of trance-inducing dancing' and they also had 'some connection to Scientology.'

It was, therefore, with a modicum of apprehension that I approached this first visit to Joan and Siegfried. I later learned from them that they harboured even more misgivings about me and my 'authoritarian' department.

There clearly was something in those dire warnings I received prior to that day, because: I came to inspect, I stopped to evaluate, and I remained to admire!

Over the next few years, after I had left the Council and set up an independent consultancy for registered home owners, I became more involved with the Peredur Trust, eventually working with them exclusively as an alternative to the retirement which I had for so long been looking forward to enjoying!

Joan and Siegfried became my dear and valued friends and somehow

Peredur became my mission. With the stalwart and dependable trustees and dedicated managers and staff, we have managed to navigate through some unexpected storms and rough waters and have in sight calmer horizons for the future which lies ahead.

Siegfried will never cease in his endeavours and, although he took up the baton alone when Joan moved to the next phase of her life's destiny, he is now fortunate to have Karin's love and support—and, hopefully that necessary element of control, when he looks to continue working his 16-hour days!

It was an honour and a privilege to be asked to write this foreword to such a valuable record of care, perseverance and success within the philosophy and teachings of Dr Steiner. From its very conception and its early beginnings you will understand the many obstacles which had to be overcome initially by those four Founders and then by Joan and Siegfried in the move to Cornwall.

Their courageous and selfless venture set the pattern for a caring and support facility for the long-term future. The stated aims and objectives of the Trust have now also been used to facilitate a provision for HIV patients at another of their sites, and so it continues...

When I stop to ponder my own involvement and the reasons why my personal lanthorn lighted my way to Peredur, I can but reflect on three mottos which had some bearing on my earlier life:

From my primary school   *je puis:* I can

My Alma Mater   *Sursum Corda—Pactum Serva:* Lift up Your Hearts—Keep the Faith

The Royal Air Force   *Per Ardua ad Astra:* Through Adversity to the Stars

I am proud to commend this book with its record of optimism and selfless service. As to the title, it does, indeed, underline Ben Sweetland's words that: 'We cannot hold a torch to another's path without brightening our own.'

Paul A. Clark

Introduction

I have been asked over time and by various people to write the story of Peredur (now working as the Peredur Trust) and that of my own life as well. It is true that it is more than 60 years now that the two have been linked together. We might look at the very beginning of the work, its manifold motivations and responsibilities as being carried by a group of four, namely Marguerite Jarvis, Lore Richter, Joan Hinchcliffe and Siegfried Rudel. But where did they come from and how did they meet? And did they all stay on throughout the years? So we will, to begin with, look at the lives of 'The Four Founders' and briefly also at our present situation.

Two of the four actually returned after a time to the work they had been doing before. The other two stayed on throughout and it seems that their earlier lives had prepared them for it. They are Joan Hinchcliffe (later Rudel) and the present writer. Joan, sadly, died on 31 May, 2003 while still engaged in planning and guiding the work. I continued working for the Peredur Trust and function now as its President. My message to present and future Members of the Trust is contained in my little speech as the outgoing Chairman and Chief Executive, at the Council Meeting on 11 December 2008.

Dear Colleagues and Friends,

What I wish to say at this juncture could be summed up in just two words:

Thank you.

Let me substantiate this.

There has been an underlying motto for the work of the Peredur Trust. It was put into words by our life-long friend and member Arne Klingborg of the Rudolf Steiner College in Jarna (Sweden). It was in answer to my rather desperate question:

'How can one, with others, be pursuing a common task and, whilst trying oneself to remain faithful to one's own ideal, yet respect the others' individual freedom?'

The brief answer Arne gave was:

'There are two pillars on which a modern social undertaking can stand.

They are **TRUST** and **RESPONSIBILITY**.'

Throughout the years I learnt to appreciate that. **TRUST** needs courage, and perhaps also the willingness sometimes to be disappointed. But it can become an enabling power. We all can grow into a new task over time and through each other. That is when Goethe's saying rings true: 'One alone can do but little. But much can be achieved if the single person will unite with others at the right time.'

RESPONSIBILITY is born when we stretch ourselves beyond our own personal selves to embrace wider aims and with which we are willing to identify. They then in turn become growing points for the Soul.

So now I say **THANK YOU** for your willingness to play each your own instrument well so that hearing the orchestra as a whole can be a pleasant experience for all concerned.

What, in the present volume, follows on from the biographical chapters, leading as they do into the beginning of the enterprise, is not what the reader might have expected, namely a historical, year-by-year account of events and activities. On the one hand this would have been very difficult if not impossible to achieve and, on the other, might not have been of particular interest to the reader. But what forms a main part of this book are the 'Themes in a Peredur Narrative and Beyond'. These themes are related as impulses arising, often in response to the situations around us. This twofoldness brings to mind these words of Rudolf Steiner's:

> Destiny is the result of two factors, which grow together in the life of a human being. One streams outwards from the inner depths of the soul, the other comes to meet the human soul from the world around him.

The varied themes often intertwine and stretch throughout the years and some into the future of the Peredur Trust. They often pervade the whole narrative in a continuing or recurring fashion, rather like musical themes can do by appearing throughout the whole composition in ever-new modulations. They might have justified the phrase 'Meeting the Needs of the Time' as part of the title. They were often experienced as adventures 'not without a hint of joy or danger'.[1]

Having said this, a 'Brief List of Events So Far' (p. 148) rounds off the themes—just for quick orientation!

We will now begin with the biographies of the two first-mentioned founders, from whom we happily have both their early autobiographies, followed then by the other two.

Notes
1. Taken from a motto for life given to his six-formers by P.C. Pike, headmaster of Launceston Grammar School, in the summer of 1968: 'It is easy to pull down or to leave alone. The real task is to evolve creatively, with just a hint of joy and danger.'

THE FOUR FOUNDERS

1. Marguerite Alison Jarvis (known as Peggy) (19.08.1915–14.04.2000)

Autobiography

Marguerite Jarvis, 1952

I was born on 19 August 1915 at 5 o'clock in the morning in Streatham, a suburb of London. I lived in a nice house with a large garden: together with my two brothers, one three years older, the other seven years younger—spent a very happy and harmonious childhood with very loving parents.

In the year 1926 when I was 11 years old my parents heard of a school which had been started very near to us called 'The New School' [later Michael Hall] run on the principles of Rudolf Steiner. My parents, who had recently left the 'Wesleyan Church' and were seeking a new teaching, visited the school and asked who Rudolf Steiner was. The school was very small and very much in the pioneer stage, but I was sent there for two years and had Mr Mann as a class teacher with four other children. Afterwards I was sent to a boarding school on the south coast of England until I was 17 years old.

On leaving school, I wanted to study music. I had been having piano lessons since the age of 6, but as it was quite impossible to get a grant in those days I decided to take an office training so that I could earn money and spend my free time studying music.

Having qualified in shorthand, typewriting and bookkeeping at the age of 19, I got a job as a doctor's secretary in Harley Street in London, continuing always with piano lessons.

Eighteen months later came a very important event. On my way to work I met Mr Mann, my former class teacher during the two years at Michael Hall School. He asked me what I was doing and when I told him I was secretary to a doctor he said, 'Come and see me this evening. We need a new secretary at Michael Hall School.' This was in 1935 when I took over the job of secretary in Michael Hall including all the correspondence and bookkeeping. Here at Michael Hall I heard for the first time of anthroposophical medicine and the Clinic in Arlesheim

(Switzerland). I became extremely interested in the medical work Dr Nunhofer was doing with the children, especially massage, and he told me of courses held in the Ita Wegman Clinic. I knew immediately that this was where I wanted to go, but had to wait patiently and save money.

After three years in the office at Michael Hall I came out to Arlesheim in August 1939 for one year, to take a course in massage, anatomy and painting with Frau Dr Hauschka, lyre playing and the study of Rudolf Steiner's *Outline of Esoteric Science* with Herr Pracht—and to learn German!

Two weeks later war broke out! I of course thought I should have to go straight back to England as long as it was possible to travel and train to be a nurse but Frau Dr Wegman, who had been Rudolf Steiner's medical collaborator, said to me, 'You should not go back to England, there are plenty of nurses in England but very few people who can be here with me—you shall learn nursing here.' So it was that I stayed and worked in Arlesheim,[1] Ascona[2] and Brissago[3] all the war years. Shortly after this talk Dr Wegman had to close her medical centre in London and needed an English person to witness her signature on the official form. She asked me to do this and then turned to me and said, 'When the war is over and you have learnt a lot about our methods of nursing you must then go back to England and help to get a medical centre going again.'

When the war was over I returned to England in 1945 to see if there was any possibility of starting an anthroposophical medical centre, but alas there were no doctors willing to do this.

After 12 difficult years mostly in curative education—Camphill and Peredur Home-School, and a very long illness—destiny led me back here in 1957. My mother very much wanted to see the Goetheanum and the Ita Wegman Clinic, so we came out on holiday to Arlesheim in August 1957. During this stay she was taken very seriously ill and could not travel back to England. She was operated on for cancer in Basel and nursed here in the clinic for nine months until she died on 6 May 1958. Of course I stayed with her, but I did not return to Peredur after her death. I had my knee permanently stiffened (it had been giving me a great deal of trouble), and was then able to do full-time nursing until 1967/8 when I began 'Lyre[4] playing with the patients'—the beginnings of Music Therapy.

During the years in the Michael Hall School office, I had once asked one of the teachers: 'Has Dr Steiner said anything about music?' The answer was, 'Yes, but it is not yet translated into English.' 'Oh, then I must learn German,' I said. Little did I know that this, in later years, would lead to 'Music Therapy' in the Ita Wegman Clinic.

Further aspects of Peggy's life (SWR)

I would like to refer to some earlier events in Peggy's life that are barely touched upon in her autobiography. Perhaps the reader will agree that they help to complete the picture of her as both a deeply feeling and strong personality. I had great respect for her myself as being one of the two older Peredur founders (while I was one of the two younger ones!).

When, in 1952, the Peredur Home School was officially opened and a Trust formed, she undertook the position of Secretary, with Joan appointed as Chairman. Her first set of minutes, in her beautifully even handwriting, are in front of me now as I write this. Equally alive in my memory is her faithfully giving out the regular morning and evening medicines to the children, prescribed by our school doctor, Dr K. Nunhofer, who was responsible for the medical work for many years. I also remember her playing the piano for the children's eurythmy exercises (see below). Her mother's sudden illness, in 1957, brought all this to an abrupt end, as she tells us in her autobiography.

There is another event in her life, which Peggy does not mention although it touched her deeply, and perhaps just because of that. In the early forties she had been working at Camphill in Scotland when a medical doctor from Czechoslovakia came for a longer visit. They soon formed a close friendship with each other and subsequently got engaged. She decided to join him on his return to Prague. Unfortunately, not only was her leaving Camphill taken as abandoning the duties she had taken on

which caused her distress, but her stay in Prague was cut short by her own sudden illness. This necessitated her lengthy return to the Ita Wegman Clinic, in Switzerland—as a patient this time. What was more, the political situation at the time made it impossible for Dr B. to leave his home country to join her. Peggy's illness, tuberculosis of the bones, persisted for a long time before she was able to return to nursing. Thus many years went by as we know from her autobiography. As their reunion appeared to be doomed the two resolved to rescind their engagement, painful though this must have been for both of them.

More about music

The present Music Therapist (2010) at the Ita Wegman Clinic has kindly supplied some further details.

In 1969 Peggy attended a six months' Course in lyre-playing, in Berlin. She then took on full-time lyre playing with patients, which she kept up until 1984. She was always very modest about it, refusing to be referred to as the 'lyre therapist'. As well as giving lyre lessons to co-workers and others she also started a lyre orchestra for up to 12 players who would often play at the four seasonal festivals, as well as on Advent Sundays, be it in the Community Hall or in some of the individual wards, taking their instruments from one to the other!

Notes
1. Where the clinic, a fully-fledged hospital, had been established.
2. A retreat with full medical facilities in a beautiful situation by the coast of the Lago Majora.
3. A home for severely disabled children in a similar location.
4. A newly developed string instrument of great potential.

2. Lore Richter (3.06.23–13.01.07)

From an Autobiography

Lore Richter, 1956

I was the second child, born to my parents in Berlin on 3 June 1923. When I was a year old we moved from the dark temporary accommodation in Moabit (it was the time of the inflation) to Zehlendorf into a newly built terraced house with a garden. I spent my childhood there, which was happy and harmonious. My elder sister was a mature and serious child; I was devoted to her. We had many children and playmates in our neighbourhood.

At that time the suburb of Zehlendorf was a beautiful region with country houses and large gardens, although our property lay on the edge of the town where there were still farms and fields. I see myself there holding my father's hand, walking by a golden field of wheat, with red poppies. We were on the way to the nearby farm where we got warm milk to drink, straight from the cow.

In the evenings we loved the twilight, when my mother would play tunes on the piano and we children snuggled up to her or sat on father's lap and followed the twilight passing into darkness. I could happily play with dolls but at other times also be rather wild. It was obvious to me that I would rather have been a boy—I often wore leather shorts and kept my hair well cropped. I didn't mind when children called after me: 'Just look there at that boy with a doll in his arms!' I am told that once when I was about three years old, my six-year-old sister was tormented by a neighbouring boy and was crying. I caught the lad by his shirt and gave him a hefty clout on the ear. He was speechless and made off. Yes, I was big and strong for my age.

At the age of five I was sent to primary school, which did not please me, for I had no interest in reading and writing, but would rather have played. In 1929 we both went to the Rudolf Steiner School in Berlin—Kreuzberg. My parents, in their search for a more meaningful life, had made a connection with and met the early proponents of the Christian Community—Rittelmeyer and Bock. It was through them that they were made aware of the Waldorf School. Now we travelled daily into the city by steam train. At first the journey was made together with my sister but soon I made it alone, when my sister's lessons took longer than mine.

The school became an important factor in our lives. The lively education, which was not at all dry or dreary, gave us both the proper 'nourishment'. We loved our teachers and had the greatest respect for some of them. The reading and writing that had been hammered into me in the primary school was soon forgotten and learnt afresh with a background of pictures and fairy tales. My class teacher was Clara Düberg, an experienced Waldorf teacher, who had been called to the Stuttgart Waldorf School personally by Rudolf Steiner. Now, for health reasons, she had come to the new and much smaller Berlin school. She had a large and loving heart. There were up to 50 children in our class! Often there were also children with 'special needs' in our class whom she would especially take under her wing. Here I may have felt, indeed half consciously, an early inclination towards a special curative education.

It is true to say that I had already met such a 'special' person in my mother's youngest sister, Aunt Lottchen, who as a result of encephalitis in babyhood had suffered subsequent brain damage but nevertheless remained a happy, childlike person. In later years she had a son who was born in a children's home not far away. When he was two years old my mother brought him into our family; so we two sisters of eight and eleven received, as it were, overnight a little two year old brother. He was integrated into the family very quickly, although my father had hesitated over taking in a 'son' whose father was unknown. However, my mother was quite ready for this new task. I was still young enough to accept the new playmate, whilst Susi, my older sister, soon became a loved and respected figure of authority for the little newcomer.

When, in 1933, the National Socialists came to power, there came an abrupt awakening from my childhood, especially when my father remarked at supper one evening: 'If this man comes to power, then that means a second world war and the closing of our school.' From that point on we lived in two worlds: the world of the school with our teachers and parents, and the outer world which became all the time more threatening.

We quickly learnt how to proceed and knew exactly how to deal with different situations. When in 1938 the school had to close its doors, I was deeply impressed with both the sincerity and courage with which our teachers said farewell to us all and conceded that the point had been reached where any compromise with the ruling powers was no longer possible. I experienced this moment as a far-reaching calling for my future. Soon after, the beginning of wartime brought me again and again to the experience of death: many of my friends and comrades died. In spite of all this I always felt myself to be protected and supported and loved life.

After the war I started my career in education. My vocation as a teacher in curative education always led me towards anthroposophical institutions. As I had a strong urge to travel into foreign lands, I went first to Switzerland, and later to England and Scotland. I was wholeheartedly a teacher and always felt a strong responsibility towards uniting with the anthroposophical endeavour.

In August 1948 I went to the Sonnenhof in Arlesheim in order to take part in a training course in anthroposophical curative education. During my earlier studies at the Stuttgart Waldorf Teachers' Seminar I had met Werner Pache, who told me about his work with the Ita Wegman Fund and suggested that there was now a possibility of receiving a scholarship for the developing curative education at the Sonnenhof. Soon after the war, whilst assisting in the Berlin School, I met many children with learning difficulties. My need to train for this task dominated the commitment that I felt at the end of the teachers' seminar. I also felt that I would still not be mature enough to take on the task of being a Waldorf School class teacher for the eight years of the lower school period. For the next step on my life's path it was important, and very attractive to me, to take the opportunity to leave Germany for the international atmosphere of Switzerland. Werner Pache represented an openness to the world which impressed me, especially after the restrictions of the Nazi time and the war.

During my course at the Sonnenhof I met many young people from all over the world. Many of us had been through difficult experiences and now found ourselves together, with our mutual interest in anthroposophy being like the elixir of life, deepening our feeling for a real curative education. Thus a strong feeling of community arose among us. We felt gratitude to the destinies that had led us to be here together. As is generally known, our training, to a great extent, involved the actual life and work with the children. The enthusiasm and devotion, which we experienced in our teachers, fired us on and helped us to overcome any difficulties

Later aspects of Lore's life (SWR)

While still in Switzerland Lore had listened to the account of one of her tutors' journey to Scotland and his visit to the Garvald Home, near

Edinburgh, which was an anthroposophical home for children and young people in need of very special care. She kept remembering that. But in the meantime, as the end of her training approached—it was in the summer of 1951—she joined the group discussions that were taking place at the 'Sonnenhof' and in the Ita Wegman Medical Centre which centred on the possibility of founding a Home School in southern England (especially in connection with the Michael Hall Waldorf School) for children who, at least for a time, would need special education in a smaller setting before hopefully rejoining a 'normal' school again. This would be a new and much-needed enterprise in which Lore became very interested. Thus she became one of the group of four who decided to work together to bring such a school into being. In the autumn of 1951 this plan was carried forward so that the Peredur Home School could start working by the end of that year. Living and working with 'maladjusted' children was of course rather new to Lore. Nevertheless, she became one of the four who started Peredur Home School.

In the following summer, in 1952, she visited for the first time the Garvald Home she had heard of earlier. It immediately appealed to her as being rather similar to her life and work at the 'Sonnenhof'. She decided there and then that this would really be her line for the future and moved there for the next four years to begin with. It was her mother's illness that then called her back to Berlin.

After her mother's death and another short spell at the 'Sonnenhof', Lore returned to working in the Garvald Home again, this time for a longer time—in fact for the next 23 years. Her friendship with the two Garvald founders, Aletta Adler and Willi Ammann, was a welcome support as she took on more responsibility. She was the Principal of the Home from 1969 until 1988. I well remember an occasion when Joan and I visited her there. It was—St Michael's Day—when Lore conducted the festive occasion of building up a beautiful harvest table with a large group of disabled residents. Each in turn was called forward both by their own name and also that of the autumn gift that each had carried in from the garden to be placed with all the others to make an impressive harvest show indeed. All this was carried through with great enthusiasm. Here are the three verses of an autumn song:

In Autumn St Michael
With sword and with shield
Passes over meadows and orchards and fields
He is on the way to battle

'gainst darkness and strife
He is the heavenly warrior
Protector of life.

The harvest let us gather
With Michael's aid
The light he sheddeth fails not
Nor does it fade
And when the corn is cut
And the meadows are bare
We'll don St Michael's armour
And onward we'll fare.

We are St Michael's warriors
With strong heart and mind
We forge our way through darkness
St Michael to find
And there he stands in glory
St Michael, we pray
Lead us on to battle
And show us thy way.

In later years Lore spent much time in an advisory capacity and finally retired from Garvald in 1996. She spent the last 10 years of her life in a newly established home for the elderly in Bielefeld (Germany), pleased to meet old friends and to make new ones, even to do the occasional bit of travelling again. Only the last year she found hard to bear, after a serious stroke. Her Christmas wish to go soon was fulfilled. She died in her sleep in the early hours of 13 January 2007.

3. Joan Rudel (nee Hinchcliffe)
17.05.1915–31.05.03

SWR

Joan Rudel, 1945

Joan Rudel was born on 17 May 1915, in Paignton, Devon. A sister was born two years later. The parents soon moved to Cornwall where Joan grew up, first in St Austell and then in Lostwithiel. Her mother had come from Redruth in Cornwall. Her father, who hailed from Yorkshire, was a pharmacist. He would often take Joan, as a little girl, into the flowering meadows nearby and teach her the names of wild plants.

A sudden change occurred when Joan was 16. Her father's mother was taken seriously ill and the family moved to Yorkshire. That is how Joan came to meet anthroposophy. She attended the High School for Girls in Leeds where Eileen Hutchins, who later founded Elmfield Steiner School, taught for just one term. A group of the Upper Sixth girls were invited on occasions to the house of Muriel Golding, another teacher, to attend anthroposophical talks. Joan, who was then in the Lower Sixth, was invited too. She remembered especially Mrs Plincke's lectures on 'The problem of evil in Goethe's *Faust*' and 'The problem of evil in Dostoyevsky's *Crime and Punishment*'. Coming away from one of them, she said to herself: 'This is the way I want to go on.'

On leaving Leeds Eileen Hutchins moved to Sunfield, the first anthroposophical home for handicapped children in this country. This led to a visit there by a group of Leeds University students of whom Joan was one. She was enthusiastic about the way in which Art and Music and the love of nature pervaded the life at Sunfield. She wanted to join it straightaway but Fried Geuter, one of the founders, advised her first to finish her degree course (in English Literature). This she did. She felt that the five years or so which she did then spend at Sunfield gave her most important impulses for the future. The seasonal plays written by Michael Wilson and Fried Geuter remained deeply engraved in her memory.

Maria Geuter's detailed knowledge of gardening, cooking and baking gave Joan a foundation for much of her practical work in later life.

Joan was at Sunfield when Dr Ita Wegman visited there after the Bangor Summer School, together with a group of active anthroposophists. Among them was Caroline von Heydebrand, one of the original Waldorf teachers. Another was Werner Pache, that early curative teacher, whom she then met for the first time.

The onset of the Second World War seriously disturbed the life at Sunfield. Joan went to teach for a year at a school in Leicester. She also spent some time with friends in Cambridge. It was there that she received a letter from Cecil Harwood asking her to come and teach at Michael Hall School (then at Minehead in Somerset). She accepted that and it gave her life a new purpose. In due course it led to her helping to found a new school in London, together with Kate Elderton. However, this was a particularly difficult time during the last year of the war, and in 1944 the school had to close because of the 'flying bombs'. Just before that happened Joan had had a letter from Morwenna Bucknall, with whom she had shared accommodation in Minehead, inviting her to visit Camphill, a home near Aberdeen, for children with special needs. She took that up— and stayed to work there for six years. That is where I met Joan, for the first time, in the autumn of 1948. Joan was both teaching as well as

Joan in conversation with a colleague at Camphill, Aberdeen, 1948

carrying care responsibilities. The care of the land was also close to her heart.

During that time we often had long and searching conversations, sometimes deep into the night. The ethos of taking care of those less fortunate than ourselves became a reality. When we both left Camphill in the summer of 1950 the foundations had been laid for a future working together. Our concern was particularly for those youngsters who did not thrive in an ordinary school and/or their home situation. They might be enabled to do so after a time at a carefully planned and multi-faceted school, as well as 'home' life. Hence the eventual designation came to be 'Peredur Home School'. When we had left Camphill we both spent a year at the 'Sonnenhof' near Basle where Joan could practise her German in a new teaching situation.

This was altogether a seminal year. We met several of the early pioneers who had worked with Rudolf Steiner. Meetings took place at the Ita Wegman Clinic, a new anthroposophical medical centre nearby where our new-found group of four discussed the possibility of returning to England in order to start a school especially for those 'borderline' children some of whom were then becoming known as maladjusted. Such a school could, perhaps, work in collaboration with Michael Hall School, the first Steiner Waldorf School in Britain, founded in 1925. At the 'Clinic' Joan had also met Mr and Mrs Allan again, the parents of a previous pupil of hers at Camphill. They offered to lend us the money to start if Joan would take on the care of their boy again.

Looking back to that moment in time it is symptomatic that among the active participants at the official opening of Peredur Home School in East Grinstead on 2 February 1952 there were present: Mr A.C. Harwood and L.F. Edmunds from Michael Hall School, the first Steiner Waldorf School in Britain; Fried Geuter from Sunfield, the first special needs home in Britain, based on an anthroposophical approach; Dr Margarethe Kirchner-Bockholt from the Ita Wegman Clinic in Switzerland; and Dr Portia Holman and Dr Marjory Franklin from the Council of the newly founded Association of Workers for Maladjusted Children, which we had already joined. (See photograph p. 45.)

As far as Joan's earlier life is concerned my account so far may have given some of its key points. It could be said in a way that from this point onwards Joan's life and the life of Peredur became one.

However, before going further with this story I would like to stay with this beginning phase for just a little longer. The question may already have occurred to the reader: How was it possible that the

Peredur Home School sprang into life so quickly? In fact, we had even been able to take the first children into our care already in the first week of December 1951, which was two months before the official opening! Excerpts of some of the letters that had flown hither and thither earlier may illustrate the urgent need to provide for these borderline children, which was felt at that time by many people. Here is the first letter, written in March 1951, *from Joan Hinchcliffe at the Sonnenhof, Arlesheim, Switzerland, to Francis Edmunds, at Michael Hall School in Forest Row, Sussex, where he was teaching.*

Dear Mr Edmunds,

Perhaps you will remember that when you were in Camphill to discuss the question of the standing of St John's School (*part of Camphill, Aberdeenshire*) you spoke of the need for a home for 'borderline' children in the south of England. I was most interested in the question, because I had worked with so many of these children in Camphill. At the time of our talk I was even on the point of saying to you straight away that I would like to help with such a home, but of course I was still a member of the Camphill Community and not in the position to make such an independent suggestion.

But now, since I have left Camphill, it has come about that I and two other teachers ... would like to come to England, to make a small home for such children. There is also the possibility that someone will buy us a suitable house and grounds near Michael Hall, if you, as a school, would feel able to give such a small home your support. I think it would be good if we could work in a rather close connection with you, to take in 'problem' children of yours, and also to send children who were able to take part to certain school lessons. We would so far like to limit the number of resident children to 20.

The people who are thinking of buying the house want to live near and make themselves responsible for the bio-dynamic upkeep of the garden and grounds, so that we would be able to work entirely with the children ...

Francis Edmunds, from the Waldorf School, Stuttgart, where he was visiting, to Joan Hincliffe March 30th 1951.

Dear Miss Hinchcliffe,

Your very interesting letter reached me after the end of term meetings and just as I was launching into our annual meeting of the Association for Teachers—and the minute that was over I left for here ... I do not know quite when I shall get back home—but the College will in any case not meet before Monday, April 23rd.

Your suggestion goes fully in the direction I have had in mind for some time. I certainly would welcome it. Whether, however, the rest of the college will think with me, I cannot say. The matter will need thinking over very carefully down to certain details, above all in connection with the basis on which you will receive children.

Out of interest I attended an inaugural meeting for the founding of an Association for Workers with Maladjusted Children. To my surprise I was elected on the interim committee and am now on the permanent committee—for the Association has now been founded. I have already made some interesting connections and will be in a good position for finding out what other people are doing and how they manage it.

As regards help from the state, the only help about which I am fairly sure is that you will get children—and the state pays well for them. I do not think matters have developed sufficiently far for any hope of capital help as yet. If the College should be willing to back the scheme, so that I can tackle the matter with some force behind me, it might be worth trying—but I should not count on it at present.

You will be interested to hear that Michael Hall will shortly have a full page article with photographs in the *Times Educational Supplement*. The *Times* representative wrote the article after a visit and allowed me to see and at some points to modify the proofs. This is the direct fruit of the Exhibition we held in London last Autumn.

With kind regards, yours sincerely, L.F. Edmunds.

Francis Edmunds, from Forest Row, to Joan Hinchcliffe, at the Sonnenhof, Arlesheim, Switzerland, 4 May 1951.

My dear Joan Hinchcliffe,

Many thanks for your letter of April 27th, with all its details.

I am very glad you will be coming over on May 10th. If you would like us to put you up here for a night or two, please let me know.

My colleagues remain keenly interested in the idea in general and look forward to hearing further about the place you have in mind, your final group of colleagues and the degree to which we can envisage co-operation.

Yesterday I had a visit from the Director of Education for East

Sussex. He stayed for about three hours and we talked about several matters. I spoke to him at some length about the ideas I have had with regard to the kind of school you now have in mind and he was extremely interested. He said that his Council would not be in a position to offer capital for building but he was absolutely sure that you would have all the children you could wish and was prepared, when the time came, to insert notices about the opening of such a special school in appropriate places. He thought it would be a good thing if I saw someone at the Ministry and he mentioned a Miss Young, with whom they have correspondence. He even said that he thought for special schools the Ministry might consider giving funds for building ...

(This was in fact the case in the eighties, when we were already settled in Basill Manor, Cornwall. The then Department of Education and Science enquired whether the Peredur Trust had a project for school leavers in need of support and which needed funding. We described our plans for refurbishing the Mill house at Basill Manor as a craft workshop, which they approved of and, after inspections etc., paid half of the rebuilding costs. *S.W.R.*)

Francis Edmunds, from Forest Row, to Joan Hinchcliffe, 13 June 1951.

My dear Joan Hinchcliffe,

... I went up to London last Thursday and had one-and-a-half hour's conversation with Mr. N. who is the Secretary at the Ministry dealing with problems of maladjusted children. It was a most interesting talk. The gist of it is as follows: He anticipates no difficulty about starting such a school ... He thinks also there will be no difficulty about children and numbers. The idea of informing the various authorities as soon as possible of the actual date of opening would be good. If the time is given in advance there is no reason why you should not have the pupils you need for the opening date ...

Joan Hinchcliffe to Francis Edmunds, 19 June 1951

Dear Mr Edmunds,

Thank you for your letter of the 13th.

We are very glad you have met Mr. N. and made such a good contact with him. Even if the Ministry cannot help us with a grant at the moment—and we actually had not much hope that they would—it is very useful to have all this information. As you say, we can always raise the question with them again when we have established ourselves independently ...

Claire R. to Joan Hinchcliffe, from Carlton Hill, London.

Dear Joan,

... I have a class of twelve very happy children. One of these children, a fat little fellow called Geoffrey, should really come to your new school. His mother is writing to you and I do hope you will be able to take him ... There might also be a bigger boy in our school who should come to you ...

(Excerpt from a London schoolteacher whom we had recently met again. It is worth noting that Geoffrey became, in fact, one of the small group of children who 'started the school' already on 1 December 1951! *SWR*)

So much for the earlier correspondence.

In this connection another question that might arise is: Why was 'Peredur' chosen as the school's name? Here the name of Violet Plincke should again be mentioned because it was she who said, when the question of a name came up in conversation in the Allan's house, 'Why not call it Peredur?' 'What is Peredur?' we asked. We learnt only then that it is the Welsh name of and synonymous with 'Parzival' in Wolfram von Eschenbach's epic of the twelfth century and in Richard Wagner's music-drama called *Parsifal*. He first became a Knight of the Round Table and then, leaving the Round Table, the undaunted seeker of the Holy Grail. Violet Plinke had already written to Joan on 13 June 1951:

... The stronger your impulse and fidelity of determination, the more you will find new human beings drawn towards the task you set yourself ... Of course nobody can expect that everything leading to the full realization of your plan will run absolutely smoothly and easily, but you have all ... gone through so much that you are equipped with armour and weapons of the Spirit—so no Fear can come near you ...

After 50 long years of Peredur work we can now look back on Joan's major share in it. So let this chapter of her biography be ended with three contributions which were written about Joan when her earthly life had come to a close. They look back on her life and work with great thankfulness.

Alan Brockman, an old farmer friend of ours, remembered:

... A group of four returned to England to found Peredur Home School, in 1951. This was in the neighbourhood of Michael Hall and for what were then called 'maladjusted' children.

Peredur not only had a large garden but also some farmland as well and biodynamic work started in earnest. Their experience led to the conviction that biodynamically grown food really helped the development of children.

We had acquired Perry Court Farm in 1953, then a mainly fruit and arable farm and it was not long before Joan, whom I had met about that time, was encouraging us to grow fruit and vegetables bio-dynamically for Peredur. One can honestly say that it was largely due to this that the bio-dynamic work here was started and enabled to expand.

Over the years Joan's unfailing support for the biodynamic impulse led not only to Peredur taking on more land (the original 20 acres growing in time to 230 acres) and livestock including a milking herd, but also to a whole range of related activities. These included: a farm shop, a milk delivery round which also included fruit and vegetables, the forming of a little group of five farms which were able to keep this supplied, a bakery with bread made from wheat grown on the farm and fruit juice production from apples and soft fruit. All this work went on whilst the main activities with the children continued apace. This led to: a pottery, a weavery, a publishing company (the Lanthorn Press) and much else. We have to thank Joan and Siegfried Rudel for making Maria Thun's *Planting by the Stars* Calendar available to the English speaking world. Their dedication over 26 years included not only the translation but also the publishing of this important research and development work. This was all done on a voluntary basis—a true gift and labour of love bringing biodynamic ideas to many. This work is now shared by others.

In addition to all this Joan and Siegfried hosted the annual conferences of the Experimental Circle for many years both at Peredur in East Grinstead and later, when they moved to Trebullom. This served to consolidate the biodynamic work and its core of members who had rarely the chance to meet as a group. Many memories spring to mind, very human and sometimes dramatic! Throughout there was always a sense of festivity—a real festival for our work.

Joan had a deep connection with the Arthurian stream which leads on to the 'Quest for the Grail'. This brought the name Peredur (the Welsh form for Parzival) to the school together with a beautiful mural connected with it. It was not therefore so surprising that when Peredur had to move (because of a threatened bypass close by) the Tintagel area became the new scene of activities.

This again led to intense activity on three sites, at Trebullom, at

Basill Manor and on Tregillis Farm. Again biodynamic work was fostered and now on an even bigger scale. In fact the emphasis began to swing more to older trainees and land work so the farm became a focus of attraction together with biodynamic studies with local people.

One feels it is not for nothing that Tintagel and its environs had such impulses brought to it. Maybe the legend that King Arthur lies sleeping in the hills awaiting the time to reawaken really points to something! In impulses behind biodynamic work we can find the cosmic Arthurian aspect. We need to awaken to these coming from above to really understand and work with biodynamic agriculture—a truly holistic view is called for. Surely Joan could be considered as a modern-day representative of this Arthurian awakening.

Christopher Clouder wrote:

Joan has been a great influence on me throughout my life and, as my aunt, took a beneficent and supportive interest in all my work on behalf of and within Steiner Waldorf education and anthroposophy. She made it possible for me to be at Michael Hall as a student in the Upper School and her work at Peredur inspired me to become a teacher.

She took on her tasks in life with single-minded purpose and devotion. Her generous impulses and strong will were part of a personality who was able to turn to many aspects of life and achieve a great deal in her lifetime. Peredur stands at a significant and inspiring step forward in helping young people with special needs and in its time has assisted many of them to find a fruitful and fulfilling path in life.

Her passionate interest in the environment and educational issues led her to meet and work with many other gifted and thoughtful people, and she was able to put these friendships to good use in successfully following her own idealistic goals in many different areas.

I sorely miss her wise and loving advice as well as her lively questioning interest and kindness.

And finally what **Eric Fairman** called 'A Tribute to Joan Rudel':

Joan was a lady who possessed her own very clear pictures of how present and future undertakings should develop. This clarity of thought and the accompanying ability to express her opinions endeared her to many, whilst others were challenged by her outspokenness. I am one of the former majority who had the extreme good fortune in meeting Joan more than 50 years ago. It was when, as a 12-year-old 'tearaway', I was placed at the Peredur Home School by the local authority. I have been blessed with her friendship, clear thinking and mentorship ever since.

My three years at Peredur were all too short, but the seeds that had been sown and nurtured during that brief period are lasting me a lifetime. Only those of us who were welcomed from the 'cold' of a sterile state children's home into the 'warmth' of Peredur can appreciate what it meant to receive not only physical nourishment, but also that all-important 'soul' nourishment. The candle, the evening prayer, the regular mealtimes, the grace before the meal, the jam and preserve making, the bread making, the gardening, walks, the Sunday Children's Service, the celebration of the seasonal festivals, together with thoughtful admonishment for wrongdoings, all helped to nourish us in ways that we had never before experienced. Which school would these days start a 'farm' to meet the needs of one individual boy? A boy who would eventually become a Waldorf teacher in his own right.

A few weeks prior to her passing into the spiritual world, Joan telephoned me at my home in Tasmania, Australia. She spoke with her usual enthusiasm about the plans for ongoing and future developments at the Peredur Farm and Craft Centre, now the Peredur Trust. That was typical of Joan. She gave her 'all' in the interests of those in her care and I have no doubt whatsoever that Joan will continue her work from her new abode, for as she would say: 'There is still much to be done.'

4. Siegfried Rudel (b. 09.12.1928)

Autobiography

Part One: Early years and the shadows of war

Siegfried Rudel, 1948

I was born, later than expected, at 12 o'clock on Sunday, 9 December 1928. The family lived then in the manufacturing town of Glatz, now named Klodzko, in Silesia (south-eastern Germany), but now, since 1945, part of Poland. While its mountainous ridges form the watershed north-westwards to the North Sea and the Baltic they also do so south-eastwards via the Danube to the Black Sea.

I was the youngest-born of five boys, of whom the three older ones had been born to my father's first family and whose mother had died at the birth of the third. We grew up together very much as one united and harmonious family. My mother was even particularly close to the youngest of the three, much as if he had been her own child. His early death in the war, years later, struck her particularly hard. She undertook, as an annual birthday gift for my father, who was a devoted teacher himself, to present him with the past year's record of the life and development of his two youngest children. This always pleased my father immensely and these three volumes are now—miraculously—in my hands. Here are two events in my early life described by her, one only briefly and the other in more detail. The first is an early attack I had of a severe pneumonia at the early age of eight weeks when my temperature rose to 40°C (104°F) which contrasted sharply with the frosty weather outside of over 41°C below zero (−43°F). However, I lived through it without ill after-affects and stood up when eight months old and was walking safely at 14 months. That was when our family's move was being prepared. It took us from Glatz to Lauban (now Luban), further north-west but still in Silesia, not far from the beautiful Riesengebirge (the Giant's Mountains) which later allowed for adventurous family outings right up to the ridges that now form the border between Poland and the Czech Republic. This family move was in connection with my father having been asked to become a school inspector. Thus the second incident happened in our new sur-

Still a toddler in a happy family, long before the War

roundings, where the town pleasantly tapered away into open country-side. I was two and a half years old then when, once again, I had dis-appeared. I had obviously ventured further than usual, presumably because the nearby shopkeepers had been asked not to encourage my further wanderings by giving me titbits whenever I called. It was on the way to the town then that I had been met by a young woman who having heard of my wanderings had asked the wayward little fellow: 'Are you the little Rudel?'

'No.'

'Aren't you Siegfried?'

'No, Hoppela.' (That's what I called myself then.)

Still puzzled, she had picked me up and carried me with her hoping to find out where the 'foundling' belonged and—lo and behold—she had guessed aright. That is when eventually she met up with my mother who was delighted, of course, but apparently rather alarmed at my appearance, all dirty and dusty with chocolate smears abounding, and one hand still firmly clutching the latest gift of chocolate beans. What then was my mother's summing-up of the affair when she came to write it up in her book? Quite philosophical! 'I am sure, you will get somewhere in your later life, the independent little adventurer that you are.' What a trusting mother to have had!

Another episode at six and a half was of a more sombre nature. Two years previously I had accompanied my mother on her visit to my grandfather's grave and now I had asked whether I could go by myself to the local cemetery, which I had located in my wanderings. When asked on my return what I had been doing there the answer, apparently, had been, 'Well, what you do in a cemetery. Don't you remember?'

'And what did you pray then?' my mother had probed further, and I had whispered into her ear, 'That the good God in heaven would also look after those who had died.' On the following day, quite suddenly, when sitting at the table I had come out unexpectedly with, 'I am worst off. You will all die and I will be left all alone.'

But such moods would not last very long. What troubled me more acutely was a severe inflammation of my left ear over quite a long period, which made me lose my hearing on that side almost entirely. Months of painful treatments were of no avail. Apparently I bravely weathered the long and varied treatments without complaining. But my sleep was violently disturbed over a long period when, in the middle of the night, I would suddenly start shouting and walking around agitatedly without waking up. Only various sedatives slowly helped to quieten me down. What at last helped quite suddenly and unexpectedly was a fierce attack of

My parents, before the War

measles with a high temperature. This had an immediate positive effect and improved my hearing. What also helped—in the long run—was a holiday by the Baltic Sea, long advised by the doctor and unexpectedly made possible for the five of us through a generous gift (the other two brothers having made their own holiday plans). We were even able to repeat this holiday treat in the following year. But a strange thing happened on that second return journey. It was 2 August 1934. When changing trains in Berlin, the otherwise busy metropolis was eerily quiet, with flags at half-mast everywhere: President Hindenburg, our head of state, had died. That scene struck me deeply. It was like a premonition of a dark future. Of course, what became clear only later on was the fact that his position was never filled again and Hitler, as Chancellor, assumed the position of head of state.

That brings me to the beginning of the Second World War. Occasioned by my father's health problems, our family had, in the meantime, moved north-eastwards to the smaller town and district of Lüben (now Lubin), in the lowland near the River Oder. It was there, on 1 September 1939, that I remember my mother entering the children's room looking white-faced and aghast, speaking in a toneless voice: 'War has broken out.' Simply that. No more. I do not know how we reacted. I seemed quite unable at my stage of life to appreciate the impact that this might possibly have on our own peaceful lives. But it was as if at that moment my mother had a foreboding that before the end of that war all of our lives would have changed dramatically in that we would have lost our home and four members of our close-knit family. It has to be remembered that my mother had already lost her youngest brother, of whom she had been very fond, in the First World War. That, by the way, had been the reason why I had been given the name 'Walter' as my middle name. Apparently I had looked very much like him as a newborn child.

My mother's premonition became a reality all too soon when in January 1942 my oldest brother was killed in action at Smolensk near Moscow and only four months later my second brother, too, who died at the Russian front near Charkow in the Ukraine.

My parents were most deeply shocked, and my youngest brother and I could at first hardly grasp what had happened. My father soon established a kind of memorial meeting on occasional Sunday evenings when we would gather together to remember the two oldest of my brothers who had had their earthly lives brought to an end so suddenly. We would put up their photographs, and bring flowers, light candles, play music, read from their letters, and shared poems and meditations for them who had gone before us. These occasions became even more deeply felt when, a year later, my third brother, at the age of 20, also died in action, his plane being shot down in southern Russia. He was the one to whom my mother had been particularly close and who was very open to spiritual matters. 'It is only now,' he had written, 'since Eckart's death' (the oldest brother who had died first) 'that I live more and more consciously. Only now do I become more aware of life as a whole and its continuance after death.'

Now we had three of my brothers in the other world. The reality of a spiritual world was ever more strongly brought home to me through these experiences. There was one verse that especially struck me at this juncture and which was headed 'The One Who Has Died Speaks'.

> In radiant light
> 'Tis there I feel the power of life.
> For death hath wakened me from sleep—
> From Spirit sleep.
> Oh, I shall be and do from out of me
> What radiant power
> Within me shines.

The underlying mood in the family was changing and becoming more and more serious. It was not only because the war was taking a disastrous turn for the German troops. It was also because the fanatical attitude of the Nazi Party's agents was becoming more and more threatening. My father had to stand up to them repeatedly. It was known, of course, that he was the only school inspector in the region who was not a member of the Party. Another fact was that since Berlin was under frequent air raids and schoolchildren were evacuated, whenever possible, my parents were now sheltering the two children of a half-Jewish family whom they had befriended. I remember one particular incident that could have had disastrous consequences. One of these two children, a girl, reported that at their next Hitler Youth meeting each would have to confirm, among other things, that they were of Aryan descent. What was the girl to do? 'You have to tell the truth,' my father was strong enough to say. 'We will stand by you.' We were highly tensed up as we awaited her return from that meeting. And there she came, bouncing down the garden path: 'As my turn came up in the queue the agent filling in the forms did not always wait for all the answers and just ticked my "Aryan" box murmuring the word to herself as if I had said it!' Care had to be taken at school as well. I remember telling my mother that my Grammar School class was split just about down the middle regarding our political stand; some quite accepting the Hitler regime and others keeping themselves clear of it where ever they could. My mother anxiously urged me not to let on what our stand was.

Another earlier incident. One Sunday afternoon I was playing on the floor in the far corner of our sitting room when my father—obviously unaware of my presence—was speaking earnestly with some of his friends and coming to the point of wrestling with the question: How could God have allowed such a regime to take hold of the nation? Or has it been inflicted upon us in order to test us?

My father's strong inner life was a help to me through many an earnest conversation. I also became aware of the fact that he did not only keep office correspondence on his desk, but also, sometimes, in one corner, verses for meditation. I copied one and it meant much to me for years to come.

Part Two: Through chaos onto new ground

Early in 1944 my brother Harald, then just turned 18, had been called up to serve in the army in the north-west near the Dutch border. Thus Christmas 1944 was a sombre affair with just the three of us, although we kept it as we always had done for 'The Twelve Days of Christmas'. In early January then when my parents packed away the Christmas decorations, candleholders, etc. my father said pensively, 'Strange to think— will we be unpacking them next year?' No more than a fortnight later we were housing the first refugee from the East. What is more, on the evening of that day my father was served notice to report for duty, early the very next morning, in the hastily formed *Volkssturm* (People's Force). My father was dumbstruck. My mother wrote later, 'He stood there deathly pale and unable to move or say a word, it was as if he foresaw the cruel events that were coming.' I was also called up, albeit to a different unit—my father because he was in his 60th year and I because I had just turned 16. The three of us were still able to meet just briefly once or twice more before my father's unit was moved to the front line further east. From there we heard no more.

Being stationed in the local army barracks it was possible for me to drop back home intermittently to see my mother and keep her up with the latest news. It was in the night of 27/28 January 1945 that things came to a head. We could hear the gunfire from Steinau on the River Oder and were given orders to move west, inadequately equipped as we were. I quickly went home to pass on that news and that we were likely to be disbanded soon. I also fetched my brother's bike for my own journey—it was better than mine! That gave my mother the signal to move from her home too. She had been hesitating as long as I was still around. Later in the night she was spotted by some of my fellow-travellers pushing her bike through the deep snow, with her little dog looking out of her rucksack and other luggage dangling from her bike. 'There goes Siegfried's mother,' one of my fellows called out as they were overtaking her in the endless stream of refugees. She heard it and called, 'Is he with you?'

'No, he has gone ahead to find quarters for us in the next village.'

'Tell him that I am making for Haynau, to our relatives!'

That was a wonderful stroke. I had no further duty with my emergency unit, in fact it had ceased to exist and I had already 'lost' my gun in the deep snow in the nearby forest. We met in Haynau not very much later and could think—what now?

We remembered that Fanny Paul, a friend of the family and a keen student of anthroposophy, who lived in Dresden, had said to us some time ago, 'Should it ever be necessary for you to come away from Silesia, then you can come to me'—as if she had had visions of the future! So we decided to try and make our way to Dresden, a distance of some 80 miles. I do not remember how we managed that. But the warm welcome we were given I have not forgotten. However, it was only days before our spell of peace was broken. For then the disastrous Dresden air raids struck. For many a dark hour we would then sit with our hostess in her cellar following on the radio the approaching bombers, wave after wave, and hearing the tremendous explosions. Luckily, the houses at the outskirts were spared. But as we peered out we saw the centre of the town lit up from above by the slowly descending dozens of phosphorescent 'mushrooms' which exposed the town to their eerie brilliance. Not realizing that this was the first of three successive raids, I went out to help in the grounds of the furniture factory opposite 'our' house, to move from the spreading fire what could quickly and safely be moved. In the early hours of the morning there came out of the town a long stream of people with terror-struck faces and smoke-drenched clothing, making their way into the open from the ruins behind them.

Fanny Paul was now very anxious to find out what had happened to her friends and their dwellings. I offered to come with her, so we went on our bikes as far as they could carry us. It was a harrowing experience with only a very few people about, searching. One sight was particularly terrifying; it was a publishing business our friend had known well, now reduced to rubble, only the cellar left with the enormous rolls of paper—waiting to be printed, I presumed. They were now reduced to gigantic cylinders of fiery red glow, sending out such heat that we could not get anywhere near them. What of the people? I do not remember what Fanny Paul was able to find out, only that she was most deeply shocked. When we came back she took to bed with a high temperature. Naturally, we were most alarmed and anxious to find a doctor. Our hostess had mentioned the name of her doctor and we managed to contact him. He was conversant with anthroposophical medicine and actually had known Rudolf Steiner, as I found out later. 'Scarlet fever' he diagnosed. 'Yes,' he explained when we showed amazement, almost disbelief, 'you can develop scarlet fever through extreme shock.' What was more, within a few days, although she was given the prescribed medicines and all the care we could manage, she died—we had no time to think of ourselves. How could we manage to take care of the body and make a funeral possible? Again, Dr Magerstädt was most helpful and even put us in touch with Eduard Lenz, a priest of the Christian Community, who gave us great support. He had been given compassionate leave to look for his two daughters whom—alas!—he had not been able to find in the ruins of their house. Later, he himself was taken prisoner by the advancing Russians and died in tragic circumstances, on his way back from imprisonment in Siberia.

Leaving my own situation on one side for the moment, I should briefly refer to the aftermath of those days of horror that left Dresden citizens with a sense of lasting shock, the effects of which even reverberate into our own time. In the summer of 2010, at a Goetheanum conference in Switzerland, I met a Dresden citizen whose mother had witnessed the three successive air raids and who now lives in the city herself. This is how I learnt of the latest report by a Historic Research Commission published on 17 March 2010, after several years of work. They have come to the conclusion that the original estimate of dead in the Dresden air raids in February 1945 was correct in being given as 25,000. That includes the large number in refugee trains at Dresden Central Station. I learnt, through this recent unexpected meeting, of the present-day remembrances carried on by today's Dresden citizens. The first and most disastrous of the three attacks began at about 10 p.m. on 13 February 1945. This is when—right up into our own time—all Dresden church bells are rung. Also on that evening special performances are given, usually of one or the other of the Requiems of Mozart, Brahms or Verdi, or other solemn music. No one applauds on these occasions, all rise in silence including the performing musicians. Tickets for these occasions are said to be always sold out. On that night too, even during the later years of Communist rule (Dresden was part of the 'East Zone'), processions have been held with lighted candles being carried from one surviving church to another one that still lies in ruins. This is recognized as having been a precursor of the powerful peace processions in 1989 which led up to the great turning point of that year and to the fall of the Wall which had split the country into two halves all too long.

Returning to my own life experiences in early 1945, I remember a feeling of bleak nothingness I had never known and in which these latest events had left the two of us.

Once again, the question for my mother and me was—what now?

It was clear that we could not presume to live on in a flat that was not ours. We had managed to escape from the threats of the East and only just avoided a disaster from the West. What about trying the south? But where could we turn? Would it perhaps be possible to join the new streams of refugees, for which the local authorities were anxious to organize trains scheduled to take them to the south-west of the country, into parts largely untouched by the war? All the homeless people were assured that accommodation would be found for them. Vague though it was, we grasped the chance to find a home. It was a journey of some hundreds of miles before our transport reached the scheduled area in south-west Bavaria. As families were being allotted to individual homes or farms it would have been a bold assumption of course to have expected a warm reception on the part of our enforced 'hosts'. On the contrary, it almost resembled a cattle market with us refugees in the ring and the locals taking our measure before volunteering any offers! We were lucky in being allotted accommodation with a friendly couple of locals whom, we assured them, we could help in house and garden. So we settled in their modest dwelling where at least we were kindly tolerated. That was all, of course, that we could have expected in the circumstances for the forth-coming weeks, if not months. I remember, for instance, chopping wood for hours on end but quite enjoying it, or helping on a neighbouring farm. My mother found it harder to accommodate such a drastic change and was feeling lonely into the bargain. However, we made the best of our bikes, for large and small explorations of our new and pleasantly hilly area, with the Alps looming up in the distance, some still covered in snow.

Spring and summer had gone on and found me still working on a neighbouring farm. Turning hay by hand was one of the things I had to learn, that is, giving the fork a sudden jerk while it is in the air so that the hay you have picked up falls down with the underside uppermost and feathered out at the same time. Thus you go along a step at a time and keeping up with others alongside you, so that between us we would leave an evenly turned and spread-out hayfield behind us. One of my pastimes had been to carve a chess set from bits of firewood to keep us both amused of an evening. But we could not imagine ourselves going on like that. My mother, who was getting very restless, had a new idea. That was to get on our bikes and make our way, cycling, to one of the northern provinces where we knew some of her relatives had fled to. That surely might make us feel more 'at home again' to be with them.

We began to make preparations, but it was not to be. Cycling to the nearby village to do our shopping I had my bike stolen by the wayward crowd of Polish refugees who had settled there and who just laughed when I remonstrated with them. Nor did the local American commander of the occupying unit move a finger to help me to retrieve my bike. It was gone for good, and so was the idea of cycling to a 'homely' north. But this mishap turned out not to be a mishap at all. On the contrary!

Our plans were dashed, it is true, but what else could we do? I searched the map and found that the town of Stuttgart in the neighbouring county was not too far away and was Stuttgart not the town where the first Waldorf School had been founded after the First World War? I had not yet finished my schooling in Silesia and surely I could finish it there. It is true that the Waldorf School had been closed by the Nazis, but surely it would be opening again now. My mother did not need much persuasion although we did not know a soul there. Perhaps she had hopes of contacting the Christian Community there, a modern religious movement, which she had known already in Silesia. However tenuous both our hopes were, anything would do to get out of our present aimless situation! Trains were only just running again; our plans were made, determined in purpose but lacking all details. My mother's bike we now willingly left behind and packed our possessions, as much as we could carry, and set off into the unknown—a second time in the course of one year! Our first visit was to the Waldorf School, which indeed in spite of bombing damage was going to reopen shortly. What I needed was three more years to complete my schooling to pass the *Abitur*, that is, a pass in the requisite number of A levels to qualify for university entrance. And I did want to do it in the Waldorf School. Now when we were introduced to the teacher in charge of entry applications she just went by my age and said, 'I am sorry, it can't be. This class is already fully booked.' What—after all our efforts—a simple No? It was too much for my mother who burst into tears. She had lost three sons in the war and knew not where the fourth was, nor her husband. Here had been a glimmer of hope and now that was dashed. I stood paralysed just looking at the teacher who, deeply struck and speaking with quick determination, replied, 'It's all right. We will fit him in.' I hardly knew where I was. A new door had suddenly sprung open.

Our inability to pay my school fees was also resolved in a remarkable way. The school's godfather system sprang into action and my three years' fees were paid by one such benevolent friend of the school who had finished paying for his child's schooling and could afford now to pay another pupil's fees. What is more, he became a fatherly friend for me.

As to my own father, we heard of the end of his life only after quite some time had passed, but his spiritual presence had already begun to be felt. That is expressing itself in the poem that I wrote at the time.

> Through many a day and night
> Uncertainty was mine,
> Until in heavenly light
> His countenance did shine.
>
> His image is reborn,
> Is mine again, and new.
> What could have been forlorn
> Is near again and true.
>
> And when at night I'm free
> To rise, in liberation,
> I feel eternity
> In blissful consecration.
>
> O star that lights my way,
> I feel your peace right now.
> One day I will repay
> Your love. But tell me how!

My first activity in the new school was volunteering with others, some of them future classmates as they turned out to be, to shovel the mounds of rubble that had remained from the last air raid and were obstructing the entrance to the beautifully designed school building. It had not been completed very long before the Waldorf School had been forcefully closed, in 1938. Some of my future schoolmates had been Waldorf pupils until then and some even until 1941 at the Dresden School, which had suffered closure only three years later. Some had been swept into the chaos of the last months of the war and had now come to the reopening of the Stuttgart School not just to be schoolboys and schoolgirls again, but almost like friends and allies of our teachers.

The latter, however, could not always have found teaching us an altogether easy job. At least such seemed to have been the case with our young lady eurythmy teacher who was meeting, to put it mildly, a lack of cooperation from a number of my class. I was not one of them and this not because I was just a 'good boy' but because I had always loved dancing and rhythmical movement of any kind. At any rate, our 'class guardian', an older and respected colleague of hers, had obviously agreed (perhaps in one of their weekly teachers' meetings when her class problems may have been aired) to have a word with the class as a whole. I remember him conveying his surprise that there was a problem at all—it was if anything but a phase—and even saying with quiet assurance that at this time by the following year we would most likely be one of the classes performing eurythmy on the stage at the public Arts Festival (such as took place regularly in Stuttgart). That was, of course, received by some of my friends with quiet disbelief. But—wonder, oh wonder!—he was right, and I even remember the special item we performed on that occasion. No doubt this had been greatly helped by the fact that our future eurythmy lessons had been taken on by another, more experienced and much respected lady teacher. She in fact became our friend. That was carried into effect when more than two years later we came to sit for the oral part of our *Abitur* (A levels) with all subjects being tested on the same day. We dreaded it. That was not only because of the fact that it would all be under a boiling hot July sun, but also knowing that we would be judged by local state schoolteachers whom we had never met before. True, our Waldorf teachers would be present, but only as onlookers. So now a group of our class asked our eurythmy teacher-friend whether she would do some eurythmy with us early in the morning of that fateful day. Yes, she agreed. To this day I remember the poem which she had chosen to bring to life by doing it with us, in eurythmy. It certainly gave us a measure of equanimity. Did it even contribute to the fact that none of us failed that day's exam? Be that as it may, I cannot resist sharing with the reader the amusing, if undeserved bonus that came my way a few hours later under the test heading 'German Literature'. I was given then what seemed to me an impossible task: 'Speak to us, please, about a poet of this century. But do take a few minutes to think it over!' I was completely taken aback because I could not even think of any name, let alone give any appraisal.

Then it shot into my head that, of course, as a pastime and enjoyable relief from pre-exam pressures I had in my spare time and throughout the preceding year read and re-read Michael Bauer's biography of Christian Morgenstern, and this with great enjoyment. So when I was called in again I was fully armed and with enthusiasm entered into the story of Morgenstern's life and work, in the course of which I also recited several of his poems. Little wonder that I left my examiners looking somewhat perplexed and my teachers equally surprised at my eloquence! Needless to say, my performance earned me a high grade in 'German Literature', somewhat undeserved as I said earlier.

Two special events during my three Waldorf School years were the Christmas gatherings which a group of our class prepared and to which we then also invited our teachers. I remember one such occasion when I took on the recitation of the text of the Dream Song of Olaf Asteson. This had been discovered in Norway not very long ago but originated from an earlier century. Olaf awakens from his long sleep through the Twelve Nights of Christmas and remembers his partaking in the experiences of souls after their earthly life, a dramatic and moving event. This epic may well have been known already to some of our teacher-friends but, if so, they willingly shared it with us again. Another year we asked one of them to give us a Christmas address, which he willingly did. He was our history teacher with whom I remained in contact for very many years after my time at school, which was from 1945 to 1948. Later on, in the eighties, he even came to see our Peredur work in Cornwall. We remained in touch, if only by messages, almost until the end of his life in spring 2008.

But I have jumped ahead by a number of years and need to take up the thread again, in the second half of that dramatic year of 1945, when I had found my way to Stuttgart. That is where my last brother met up with us—at last—having been dismissed earlier from his parachute regiment on account of ill health. He was once more able to take up his woodwork training of earlier years. But alas, my mother went down with severe pneumonia which kept her in the Stuttgart Bosch Hospital for several weeks. We feared for her life. When she rallied at last she did not have to return—thank goodness!—to the demeaning job of housemaid under the severe regiment of 'the Owner' simply to earn us a living but at last a pension became available for her. After a spell of recovery a new era could begin for her when the Christian Community offered her a position as a live-in house mother at their Stuttgart centre, where she could also make her home once more. I was highly relieved and so grateful that I took the opportunity of expressing my appreciation when it came my way on one of my later visits. I remember laying a bunch of roses by the door of one of the priests (on his 60th birthday!) who had been especially helpful, with a note to thank him for their 'life-saving' action in providing a long-term recovery solution for my mother.

Where had my life taken me to by then? The reader may wonder how I came to settle down and be working in England. That actually took an amusing start already in the very year that I had left school, in 1948. Always having wanted to go to Britain for a time, certainly before any start at university, I had procured the address of a London lecturer who had visited the Stuttgart Waldorf School and spoken to our class; I hoped he might help me to find a place. So I drafted a letter to him. However, at the last moment I hesitated. Having written my letter without my mother's knowledge, I felt I should let her see it at least before sending it. But I was not going to be diverted! My mother, rather splendidly and in spite of not relishing the thought of my going off to Scotland, advised me to address my letter to Dr. Karl König near Aberdeen, founder of a home for children with special needs. Years ago, he had occasionally been a visitor to our home in Silesia and would probably remember our name and, therefore, be likely to let me visit his children's home, at least for six months. Not only was I delighted to have my mother's support but I also remembered, of course, Dr König's visits and especially the nickname my brother Harald and I had coined for him. We had overheard bits of his conversations with our parents as they sat in a sheltered corner of our garden (I must have been eight or nine years old at the time). All we ever heard clearly from our family's visitor was his often repeated and emphatic statement 'Absolutely not!' So that was it: 'Dr Absolutely-Not is here again!' we would pronounce triumphantly.

But there was another, more civilized side to our connection. Dr König at that time shared in the running of an anthroposophical home for children with special needs founded by Albrecht Strohschein. This home was in Pilgramshain, Silesia, and since that was not far beyond my father's area of supervision (he was the regional school inspector) he occasionally made a point of visiting the home as he appreciated their educational— and especially the artistic—approach. He had often returned from such excursions with toys or Christmas decorations and the like, made by the children there and available for sale to visitors.

There was yet another sequel to this connection: Firstly, I must relate that the original six months of stay in Scotland that I had been granted by the immigration authorities grew to nearly two years. This enabled me, as a student, to take part in the newly formed training course in Education for Special Needs.

A visiting group of 'Curative Education' professionals came to look around the Camphill homes near Aberdeen, at Whitsun 1949. I happened to be presiding over supper with a large group of junior residents, when the door opened and Dr König brought in his visiting group of colleagues. My name must have been mentioned because a large-bodied member of the visitors' group stepped forward and greeted me: 'A son of the well-disposed inspector?' How strange it was for me to see my father's mysterious 'excursions' viewed from the other side, so to speak! I had the good fortune to meet Albrecht Strohschein again and again after this initial encounter, first by visiting him at the new home which he had started near Stuttgart after the end of the war, and adventurously having escaped imprisonment. In later years, after Peredur Home School had got going, both Joan and I met him repeatedly at conferences. He was always encouraging us to take an active part.

My final series of encounters occurred when in later years I attended meetings of the International Action Committee for Special Needs. I much appreciated these further contacts. After all, Strohschein had been one of the three pioneers of 'Curative Education'. When in 1998 the 12 lectures by Rudolf Steiner on this subject were again to be reprinted I therefore suggested that they should be prefaced by Strohschein's article 'The Beginning of Curative Education'. By the way, this was the only thing he ever wrote and that only, as I happen to know, with a lot of pushing from the coordinator of the collection of articles called *We Worked with Rudolf Steiner* (now reprinted by Rudolf Steiner Press as *A Man Before Others*).

Now back to what led to the beginning of my permanent work in England in 1951. This has already been touched upon in the earlier life-story of Joan Hinchcliffe (later Rudel), whom I had first met in Scotland in the autumn of 1948. Almost from the very beginning our working together had become twofold. On the one hand, there was the care of the children who needed a great deal of support and guidance and on the other there were the many long and searching conversations we had, not only concerning the meaning of such work but also the spiritual foundations of both our own lives. When we left Camphill in the summer of 1950 we both spent a year, as mentioned earlier, at the 'Sonnenhof' near Basle, the earliest Steiner home for children with special needs. It was here that I could continue my training in Special Needs Education. What was more, our long and searching conversations together with our two new-found 'allies' helped to crystallize our impulse to work together in starting a special school for borderline children unable to learn in mainstream schools but—hopefully—to become able to do so again after a time. The helpful talks with our new friends in the Ita Wegman Clinic continued, as did Joan's intermittent visits to England for preparatory talks with the Allans and others. As witness of this time of searching and waiting is the letter that Joan wrote to me during one of her short stays in Horsham (where the Allans lived).

> I went to Bognor Regis to see Peggy Jarvis, and we had a four hours' talk. She is quite prepared to join us, can do all office work including accounts, play the lyre and also weave. It was a wonderful talk and she has been thinking so much in the same direction as we have ... Tomorrow then, we will visit the house with Edmunds and Harwood, and afterwards Mr Allan will discuss finances with Harwood and I will talk over the remaining points with Edmunds. Tuesday, Peggy will be here ... We shouldn't be unduly optimistic, but I think that things have gone forward rather quickly. One must keep very strong and clear in one's thoughts and be in no doubt about what this school will mean. Edmunds said it will stand very much in the light of public attention,

Left to right: Dr Portia Holman (of the Assn. Of Workers for Maladjusted Children), Joan Hinchcliffe (later Rudel), L.F. Edmunds and A.C. Harwood (both teachers at Michael Hall), and Fried Geuter (joint founder of Sunfield Children's Home, Clent)

being the first school of its kind and started at this moment. But I think
Michael Hall will be very anxious to help us, and with their support,
the support of Dr Bockholt etc. and our own will to work, we need not
have any fears about taking it on. Edmunds also told me that Karl
Schubert, in his last talk with him, was very enthusiastic that such a
work should be begun in England. In fact, we are justified in believing
that a common impulse stands behind the thoughts of *all* the people
who are now concerned, including our own, and that it is the right
time. I wonder if one is also justified in connecting it with the personality of Karl Schubert. It is, actually, a continuation of the *Hilfsklasse*[1] work.

Now I think I have told you everything of importance. It would be
better not to talk about the house, even to Lore until we have actually
seen it [Very wise. It proved to be just one of several houses found to be
unsuitable!] But give her my love, and keep both of you in a positive
frame of mind!

So the search continued into the summer, yet another house was visited
and found to be very suitable. But it was sold to another interested party
without warning!

As to my coming to England, from Switzerland, there was no free
travel for 'foreigners' then! Weeks of uncertainty were hard to bear. 'I
am most unhappy about it,' Joan wrote to me on 3 August 1951 from
Horsham where again she was able to live with the Allans, while I was
still stuck in Switzerland, 'because I know things won't go in the direction they are meant to as long as we are not together. Let us keep
inwardly true to each other, and the spiritual impulse that stands
behind our intention to start this work together. I certainly will not
decide to take a house, or enter into any binding commitments, until it
is clear that you will be allowed to come over.' In the same letter Joan
gave me a full description (with sketch plan) of a large house on the
edge of East Grinstead which seemed very suitable for our needs and in
good condition. 'I think three weeks would be enough to prepare it
for opening,' she wrote. 'We will all go over ... to look at it in still
more detail. Perhaps you will be here by then. I do hope that you can
come to an arrangement to stay a week or two longer at the 'Sonnenhof'. Tell them the Home Office has not so far come to a decision,
but is trying to do so—this was also one of the phrases of the message.'
The reason for this delay dawned on me only later. In the meantime
both hopes were left unfulfilled: the suitable house was also sold to

Left to right, bottom row: Dr Marjorie Franklin, Dr Portia Holman (both of AWMC), Joan Hinchcliffe (founder, Peredur), Helen Allan (who loaned money to buy the property), Dr M. Bockholt (from the Ita Wegman Clinic). Top row: L.F. Edmunds (teacher, Michael Hall), Nimmo Allen (who organised purchase of the estate), A.C. Harwood (teacher, Michael Hall), Marguerite A. Jarvis (founder and school secretary)

another applicant of whom we had not been made aware, and my visa did still not arrive. In the meantime, money—or rather the lack of it— was becoming a serious problem. In that selfsame letter Joan told me 'I'm just writing a letter to Dr Bockholt because we *must* have more money.' The Ita Wegman Clinic had offered us a loan should we need it before we could start the work.

Eventually, 'Millfield' was found—and bought!—one mile south of East Grinstead, a very suitable main house (not too large) and two smaller ones, a large garden and 20 acres of land. It proved to be a real godsend— the right size for the beginning phase and a springboard for future development as became ever more obvious as time went on.

Both the beginning of Peredur Home School's work at the end of 1951 and its official opening on 2 February 1952 have already been described in Joan's biography, as has our connection with Mr and Mrs Allan. My life, like Joan's, was now going to become a part of the developing project.

The 'New Ground' of this second part of my biography had finally been found.

Note

1. *Hilfsklasse* = helping class. A separate initiative started by Karl Schubert in 1920, at Rudolf Steiner's request. It was a temporary learning support for children who could not at once join the class appropriate to their age in the newly founded Waldorf School in Stuttgart. Both Joan and I, each in our own way, had had the good fortune to have met this remarkable and devoted teacher. He died in 1949.

INTERLUDE

The following—more esoteric—study can build a bridge between these last two of the four biographies. However, it can be omitted if the reader prefers to press on right now to the 'Themes in a Peredur narrative and beyond'.

★   ★   ★

Going back into my early adolescent years, I recall a picture hanging up in the family's sitting room (which also served as my father's study). It haunted me. It was—as I learnt later on—a self-portrait of the Swiss painter Arnold Böcklin (1827–1901).[1] He was shown as holding a palette of paints in his left hand and a brush poised to begin painting in his right. His face was almost like that of a knight looking ahead with a firm gaze and yet, at this moment, he was as if listening to what was being said to him from behind. By whom? It was the skeletal head of Death who could be seen playing the violin, 'speaking' thus to him with eagerness from behind, his tilted head having appeared from behind the painter's left shoulder. It frightened me. But my father reassured me. 'Think not of Death,' he said, 'but rather of his angel speaking to him through his music.' That took all fear away from me.

Very many years later, when I visited Tintagel in Cornwall for the first time and again and again on later occasions, I was deeply struck by the whole setting and of the ruins that remain of an earlier castle, and of other buildings. Could I but see what happened here in the past!

Later again, I came across the description of Rudolf Steiner's visit to that site. What now follows, therefore, is taken from the chapter 'A Day at Tintagel in August 1924' from *A Man Before Others* (Rudolf Steiner Press). By way of introduction Mabel Cotterell wrote: 'Together Daniel Dunlop and Eleanor Merry arranged the Summer Schools of 1923 and 1924, choosing the centres of Penmaenmawr and Torquay. We therefore owe to them Dr Steiner's two great cycles, *The Evolution of the Earth and of Humanity* and *True and False Paths in Spiritual Investigation* ... The visit from Torquay to the Cornish coast with the ruins of King Arthur's Castle and the interplay of elemental beings in the air and the sun and the sea-spray at Tintagel, is described in Mrs Merry's delightful article below. The article describes the drive over Dartmoor but omits to say—as Dr Steiner told us—that mischievous

pixies and nixies appeared and made "long noses" as he passed! Now
to the actual article.'

'I want to go to King Arthur,' said Dr Steiner in a very resolute voice. It
was very early morning, between 5 and 6 o'clock, I think, and I heard
his firm footsteps coming to meet me in a dark passage of the hotel
when I was on my way to waken Dr Wegman as I had promised. Dr
Steiner was fully dressed, though we were not, as it was pouring with
rain and misty.

I said: 'Do you really think we can go, in this weather?' He replied:
'Why not?'—and he added: 'A few minutes after 8 o'clock the rain will
stop.'

I hurried on to waken Dr Wegman, as I had promised, and to dress
myself. By 10 past eight we had finished breakfast and, in typical
English fashion, trooped outside to look at the weather; we saw that
the mist had cleared, the rain had stopped, and the sun was shyly
appearing. So the memorable drive of some 60 miles over the heather-
covered hills began.

Nearly all the way, small fragments of rainbows seemed to descend
to the sides of the road and hovered about us as though to make our
journey a triumphal progress. It was a most wonderful sight. At last we
came again to the sea, and straight ahead of us, at the top of a grassy cliff,
were the last fragments of King Arthur's castle at Tintagel.

A deep rocky chasm divided this from a second rugged cliff, where
other remains could still be seen. We all got out of the various cars and
began to walk up the left-hand slope to the ruins. Dr Steiner was at first
silently absorbed in the wonderful view; all around was sunshine, and
fleeting cloud-shadows and little hurrying rainbows—and a stormy and
angry sea.

Between the remains of the castle and the next promontory was a
turbulent inlet of the sea. At first Dr Steiner stood, notebook and pencil
in hand, near the site of King Arthur's scattered stones. 'Here,' he said,
'were the Kitchens, and over there the Knights' quarters.' Presently he
said, 'A Knight is approaching us ...' I looked in vain, there was
apparently nothing there. It has passed from my memory what he said
further, though he described the Knight, who, I think, was not riding
but walking. He wrote other notes about the Knights' quarters and
perhaps the banqueting hall; but for the most part he was silent and
absorbed, though at the same time very positive and aware of everything.

Presently, most of us—and Dr Steiner—set out to scramble up the stony path of the opposite cliff, where there were more ruins. He said these had been the servants' quarters, and also the stables.

I do not think the cliffs can always have been divided by the chasm as now, though I do not remember Dr Steiner speaking of that. As we descended the cliff we went into what is traditionally called Merlin's Cave. Inside it there was a wonderful natural structure in which one had a good view of the shadowed rays of the sun—something like what can be seen in a Druid Trilithon, where the Druids obtained their knowledge in the shadowed shining of the sunlight.

So far as I remember, Dr Steiner did not speak about the cave, but I rather think it must have been in connection with it that he later spoke of Wagner and Merlin.

We then drove back to Torquay, and the visit to 'King Arthur' was over. But I have since felt 'in my bones' that there was something extraordinary about this visit. To what did it really refer? To England? I think not; King Arthur is too universal a figure for that. We have learned since, from Dr Steiner's lectures, that the name 'King Arthur' was the name, not of a single individual, but the name of the representative head of an Order devoted to the war against Evil, in the sense of an awakening of humanity to its inevitable and formidable presence.

There was not, of course, just one King Arthur as I used to think, but many, who were the Heads of a continuing Order of Initiates. The evil, and the social wrongs they fought against were, and are still, in another form, in our midst.

Quite recently, I came across the transcript of a lecture Rudolf Steiner gave to his colleagues at the centre of his work, called the Goetheanum, near Basel in Switzerland, describing much of his recent visit to England. I quote from it as follows:

During our recent stay in England during the Summer Course at Torquay in the West of England, not far from the place where Arthur was with his followers once upon a time (we were able to visit the actual place), a result of spiritual research was given to me, pointing to a belated working of this kind in a pre-Christian Christianity. For at this place it had indeed been preserved into a far later time. The content of the King Arthur Legend referred to in later times by a scholarship which is not at all scholarly in respect of the real facts, reaches back in reality into a very early epoch. It is indeed a deep impression which one may receive when one stands at that place, looking down into the sea even as once upon a time the Knights of the Round Table looked out upon the sea from there. Even today, if one is receptive to these things, one receives a very real impression which tells one what it was that the Knights of the Round Table of King Arthur did in their gigantic castle. The last relics of the castle, the crumbling stones, the latest witnesses to its existence, stand there to this day. Gigantic is the impression of the place of ruins, entirely broken down as it is, and from there one looks out into the ocean. It is a mountainous promontory with the sea on either side. The weather changes almost hour by hour. We look out into the sea and watch the glittering sunshine reflected in the water. Then the next moment there is wind and tempest. Looking with occult vision at what takes place there to this day, we receive a magnificent impression. There live and weave the elemental spirits evolving out of the activities of the light and air, and of the foaming waves of the sea that turn and beat upon the shore. The life and movement and interplay of these elemental spirits gives even today a vivid and direct impression of how the sun works in its own nature in the earth, and meets with that which grows forth from the earth below by way of powers and spirits of the Elements. There we receive even today the impression: such was the immediate original source of inspiration of the twelve who belonged to King Arthur. We see them standing there, these Knights of the Round Table, watching the play of the powers of light and air, water and earth, the elemental spirits. We see too how these elemental spirits were messengers to them, bringing to them the messages from sun and moon and stars which entered into the impulses of their work, especially in the more ancient time. And much of this was preserved through the centuries of the post-Christian time, even into the 9th century of which I was just speaking.

It was the task of the Order of King Arthur, founded in that region by the instructions of Merlin, to cultivate and civilize Europe at a time when all Europe in its spiritual life stood under the influence of the strangest elemental beings. More than will be believed today, the ancient life of Europe needs to be comprehended in this sense. We must see in it on all hands the working of elementary spiritual beings, right into the life of man.

The Arthurian life, as I said, goes back into pre-Christian times, and before the Gospel came there even in its oldest forms, there lived in it the knowledge, at any rate the practical instinctive knowledge of Christ as Sun Spirit, before the Mystery of Golgotha. And in all that the Knights of the Round Table of King Arthur did, this same *Cosmic*

Christ was living, the Christ who though not under the name of Christ was also living in the impetus with which Alexander the Great had carried the Grecian culture and spiritual life into Asia. There were, so to speak, later 'campaigns of Alexander' undertaken by the Knights of the Round Table of King Arthur into Europe, even as the real campaigns of Alexander had gone from Macedonia to Asia.

I mention this as an example, which could be investigated in the most recent times, to show how the worship of the sun, that is to say, the ancient worship of the Christ, was cultivated in such a place, though needless to say it was the Christ as He was for men before the Mystery of Golgotha. There all things were cosmic, even to the transition of the cosmos into the earthly Elements, the elemental spirits who lived in light and air and water and in the earth, for even in these there lived the cosmic forces. It was not possible at that time in the knowledge of these Elementals to deny the cosmic principle that they contained. Thus even in the 9th century, in the paganism of Europe, there still lived much of the pre-Christian Christianity. That is the remarkable fact. Moreover even in that time the belated followers of European paganism understood the Cosmic Christ far more worthily and truly that those who received the Christ in the Christianity that was spread officially under that name. Strangely we can see the life around King Arthur radiate into the present time, continued even into our time, placed into the immediate present by the sudden power of destiny. Thus I beheld in seership a member of the Round Table in a very deep and intense way, though he stood a little aside from the others who were given more to the adventures of their knighthood. This was a knight who lived a rather con-templative life, though it was not like the Knighthood of the Grail, for this did not exist in Arthur's circle. What the knights did in the fulfilment of their tasks, which in accordance with that age were for the most part warlike campaigns, was called by the name 'Adven-ture' (Aventure). But there was one who stood out from among the others as I saw him, revealing a life truly wonderful in its inspiration. For we must imagine the knights going out on the spur of land, see-ing the wonderful play of clouds above, the waves beneath, the surging interplay of the one and the other, which gives a mighty and majestic impression to this very day. In all this they saw the Spiritual and were inspired with it, and this gave them their strength. But there was one among them who penetrated most deeply into this surging and foaming of the waves, with the spiritual beings wildly rising in the foam with their figures grotesque to earthly sight. He had a wonderful perception of the way in which the marvellously pure sun-influence played into the rest of nature, living and weaving in the spiritual life and movement of the surface of the ocean. He saw what lived in the light nature of the sun, borne up as it were by the watery atmosphere as we can see to this day, the sunlight approaching the trees and the spaces between the trees quite differently than in other regions, glittering back from between the trees, and playing often as in rainbow colours. Such a knight there was among them, one who had a peculiarly penetrating vision of these things. I was much concerned to follow his life into later time to see the individuality again. For just in this case something would needs enter into a later incarnation of a Christian life that was almost primitive and pagan, that was Christian only to the extent that I have just described. And this in fact was what appeared, for that Knight of the Round Table of King Arthur was born again as Arnold Böcklin. This riddle which had followed me for an immensely long time, can only be solved in connection with the Round Table of King Arthur.

Thus you see that we have a Christianity tangible with spiritual touch to this very day, a Christianity before the Mystery of Golgotha which shed its light even into the time that I have just outlined.[2]

These descriptions sent me back to Arnold Böcklin as a painter. With the help of a previous colleague of mine—in the early days of Peredur Home School—I procured a biography and numerous reproductions of his paintings. They are adding life and colour to earlier intimations. To make the connection with the present time, the reader—if he or she has followed me so far—is asked to turn back now to Joan Rudel's obituary as written by Alan Brockman who makes the connection to the Peredur work at the present time. It gives substance to his final sentence: 'Surely Joan could be considered as a modern-day representative of this Arthurian awakening.'

Finally—and I add this with some hesitation—I recall the day before Joan passed away on 31 May 2003. She had asked that we should go to Tintagel once again. It was late afternoon when I drove up to where the church stands and from where, on the right, you can look across to the rocky peninsula jutting out into the sea. We stayed there in silence for quite some time, with only the sound of the murmuring sea below. As we turned to go the daylight was slowly beginning to fade.

Notes

1. *Chambers Biographical Dictionary* says: 'Swiss painter, born in Basel. His work, mainly of mythological subjects, combined Classical themes of nymphs and satyrs with dark, romantic landscapes, rocks and castles . . .' 1827–1901.
2. Taken from Lecture III, Volume IV of Rudolf Steiner's *Karmic Relationships*, Anthroposophical Publishing Company, London 1957.

THEMES IN A PEREDUR NARRATIVE
AND BEYOND

5. Special Schools—Yes or No?

This title question has given rise to lively, if not to say fierce, discussion between parents, teachers, professionals and members of the public, ever since the publication of the so-called Warnock Report and especially that of the subsequent endorsement of the integration of handicapped pupils into mainstream classes by the 1981 Education Act. Had this recommendation been turned into law too quickly or indiscriminately?

Before we quote in detail some of the points made in discussions and newspaper articles, we may ask: How had the Peredur Home School fared during these years? As the reader will remember, it had come into existence as an answer to urgent questions from teachers as well as parents. It fulfilled its task of rehabilitating pupils throughout its 28 years of working and developing, which will be illustrated more closely in some of the 'Themes' chapters later on. Suffice it to say at this stage that a number of pupils, before very long, made it back to mainstream schools again. Others stayed the full course and left as 16-year-olds, knowing now their way into life, and with the blessing of those who had been caring for them so far, both at our Home School and what was then called the Children's Departments of County Councils. Other youngsters felt less certain. They would benefit from further support, at least for another year or so, with ongoing work experience as part of their lives. Such further provision was also felt as an urgent need by a number of other special schools with whom we shared this concern, by members of the Association of Workers for Maladjusted Children, and by large and varied sections of the general public. That is why our nationwide appeal for a special building fund fell on fertile ground. We were able to raise £100,000 in the course of just one year (1964), a large amount in those days, to enable us to have a specially designed hostel built and also a number of workshops of different types. This hostel/workshop scheme was soon filled to capacity, especially since our colleagues in other special schools were pleased to use such a long-needed 'Bridge into Life' for some of their school leavers. The red Appeal brochure had spelt out the widely felt need and our detailed proposals in the first place (1964). A follow-up brochure (with a blue cover this time) now gave both an account of what had been achieved so far and what our further plans were (1970).

Before going further, it has to be noted that there were also youngsters whom, after a time, we could no longer help, largely because they were

The 'blue' fundraising brochure

becoming a danger to others. Two episodes come to mind. I remember one boy especially who suddenly turned out to be a fire-raiser, at our cost. Quick action was taken and no one was hurt. But he had to be sent away. The curious thing was that he kept coming back and hanging around in our close neighbourhood, obviously having 'escaped' from where he had been placed by the social services. The local police, of course, were not keen to have him about in their area. One particular visit of his was rather unusual. He had apparently managed to enter the girls' house during the daytime and to settle in the loft for the night. As the day just began to dawn, the girls noticed him tiptoeing through one of their bedrooms, making his way to the staircase door. 'Who are you?' one of the terrified girls managed to ask. 'Psst,' the stranger whispered, 'it's the police!' They were too frightened to do anything and just let him pass through and away. On other occasions the 'stranger' would attempt to break into the office, sometimes having armed himself beforehand with a stout poker from the kitchen! The police agreed with us that these various rather clumsy attempts could be seen as vain attempts to make himself at home with us again. But all depended on catching him at his abortive attempts in the first place. Help came when we managed to make contact with his

Play time outside the Peredur school building

social worker, one from overseas and seconded here for a year. She responded readily to our suggestion to accompany the young man in making a civilized visit to us—'coming to visit in the daytime like proper people do, and by ringing the front door bell'. He responded and did come to visit, with her having broken the ice. The old connection he had had with us was re-established and his rather weird attempts to visit ceased. But, sad to say, that capable social worker returned again to her home overseas when her year abroad came to an end. The further contact with our old friend was only renewed when we received letters from him—from prison. He was full of remorse at having landed himself there after all. We replied, of course, but it all dried up after a while.

Another, more recent story was that of a teenager who suddenly adopted the habit of fiercely punching people with his fist, quite unprovoked, be they fellow pupils or any adults, and even laughing as he did so. We were strongly advised by our social work supervisor to insist on his removal. He had to be admitted to a mental hospital, in the long term.

Returning to the provision for adolescents, this hostel/workshop scheme for school-leavers was able to function well for several years but our further forward planning had to adjust itself to changing circumstances. There were two outer aspects to that. The first was the changing environment of our East Grinstead area, 30 miles south of London, which had until quite recently been of a rural character. Housing development had gradually begun to encroach on it. But what was more, an East

Grinstead by-pass was being planned, one possible route of which would
be passing through seven fields of our farm. I remember returning from
showing a planning officer the whole extent of our work. He was honest
enough to say, 'I must confess, when we drew the line on the map we did
not realize you were underneath it!' It was in 1971 that we also began to
cooperate with a local housing association who considered that this same
route would be passing their homes too closely by far. While this threat
remained over our heads it seemed unwise to actively pursue any of our
further building plans and we began to pursue other possibilities. Should
we consider hiving off all our activities to the West Country?

The second challenge was occasioned by changing legislation in the
educational sphere. The year 1970 had seen the appointment by the then
Conservative Minister of Education of a committee 'to report on the
education of handicapped children and to make recommendations'. This
Warnock Report, in 1978, recommended the integration of handicapped
children into mainstream schools. This meant that the 'borderline' children such as were benefiting from attending special schools at present
would no longer be funded by local education authorities. Nor would
new pupils be referred to them. The Peredur Trustees therefore agreed to
bring the Peredur School activities to a gradual conclusion and to concentrate in future on the development of work with young adults in need
of ongoing support. The first new such activity in Cornwall began at
Basill Manor in 1976. This 'age-range change' marked our second
response to a changing world.

★   ★   ★

What now follows are further observations, reactions and new ideas in
response to what the *TES* (*Times Educational Supplement*), in 2005,
referred to as the consequences of 'the curious case of the Warnock
Report' (see p. 65). They are relayed for the reader by a series of newspaper articles over a number of years and will speak for themselves.

First of all, Mary Warnock herself was quoted as already sounding
certain early warnings (edited by Miriam Gross of 'Sunday Plus', part of
the *Observer*). This happened under the headline:

<h3 style="text-align:center">INTEGRATION IN SCHOOLS</h3>

**The part of the 1981 Education Act which concerns handi-
capped children came into force on 1 April. Here MARY
WARNOCK, on whose 1978 Report the act is based, considers
the problems involved.**

... Now that the integration part of the 1981 Act is to be enforced, it is high time that we asked ourselves not only who is to be integrated in ordinary schools, but who will be responsible for those so integrated. Do we believe that special schools are on the way out? Are we ready for this? ...

The aim of the 1978 report, which is the foundation of the present Act, was to widen the scope of special education so that it embraced not only children in special schools, but a further 18 per cent of children, in ordinary schools but with needs that had to be specially met, if they were to gain anything from their education. These children were not the subjects of integration; they had never been segregated. But, as top priority, the hope was that they would be given special help in the schools where they were.

It has not happened. And now they are to be joined by others who need help even more urgently ... if teachers in training could learn to take the needs of *all* their future pupils seriously; if they could be taught, by example, that teachers must work as a team, not only with one another, but with outside agencies; if, in short, they could make themselves responsible for the needs of the brilliant, the average and the retarded equally, then the ideals of the 1978 report would be near fulfilment. There would be results, not rhetoric.

There are some signs that a new generation of teachers with these ideals may be emerging: we shall have to wait and see.

We take a leap from the year of the new legislation (1981) to the time when teachers had lived and worked with it for several years, *The Times*, 17 April 2004:

INCLUSION OF SPECIAL NEEDS PUPILS 'A DISASTER'

By Tony Halpin, *Times* Education Editor

The Government's policy of educating children with emotional and behavioural difficulties in mainstream schools is a 'disaster', Britain's second-largest teaching union said yesterday.

Schools were unable to cope with violent and disturbed pupils who were a danger to themselves and others, the National Association of Schoolmasters and Union of Women Teachers said.

Children's chances were being destroyed by an 'inclusion' policy that condemned many with special needs to failure and left other pupils trying to learn in classes that were constantly disrupted. The union's conference called for special schools to be reopened as an alternative to 'enforced inclusion'.

Margaret Morgan, deputy head of a secondary school in Devon, said teachers faced classes containing numerous children with different statements of special need. She described a typical maths lesson for a class of 13-year-olds she taught. 'Student A is perfecting his animal noises, he has severe ADHD (attention deficit hyperactivity disorder) and is resisting taking his Ritalin. B is under the table because C is trying to kill him yet again. D is trying out his latest graffiti tag on anything he can find; he's statemented with severe learning difficulties—lack of writing skills. E is in tears because the division sign is on the board and she doesn't do division. She doesn't read or write either. I enjoy my job, I love teaching, and Ofsted (Office for Standards in Education) says I am an excellent teacher, but I feel more and more that I am failing.'

Sarah Cassidy, Education Correspondent for the *Independent* also writes on 17 April 2004:

More special schools must be built to prevent schools from being swamped by special-needs pupils whose disabilities and behavioural problems disrupt the education of other children, teachers say.

Forcing children with special needs to attend mainstream lessons was 'child abuse or torture' which damaged their self-esteem and disrupted the progress of other students, delegates were told yesterday at the annual conference of the National Association of Schoolmasters and Women Teachers in Llandudno, Wales.

The union voted to condemn the Government's policy of 'inclusion' and argued that the policy was putting pupils into mainstream lessons despite their disabilities, which needed the support of a special school.

The drive to close special schools and transfer pupils to mainstream education had gone too far, teachers said. Forcing mainstream schools to take children who needed specialist attention had merely turned them into 'enormous special schools without any of the benefits of true special education', the union warned.

Amanda Haehner, the union's executive member for London, said teachers were cynical about the so-called 'inclusion' policy because they suspected it was a way of saving money by shutting down expensive specialist provision. She said some children with physical disabilities or conditions such as autism, Asperger's syndrome and behavioural difficulties could succeed in mainstream classes if schools received more funding.

A week after these conference reviews, observations were made by Conor Ryan who had been special adviser to the Department of Education and Employment 1997–2001. His well-balanced article appeared in the *Times Educational Supplement* of 23 April 2004:

CHILDREN IN NEED OF A DECENT EDUCATION

Last week's National Association of Schoolmasters and Women Teachers conference called for 'inclusion' to be redefined so that more pupils with special educational needs are excluded from mainstream education. But many parents expect their children, even with complex needs, to be taught alongside their contemporaries.

This debate has always been emotional and polarized. No parents want their child set apart. For some, only a mainstream school will do. Other parents—and many teachers who have to balance the needs of the class—fear that mainstream schools can't give every child the attention they require.

But, unless we are honest about the issues, we won't find the best solutions. That means distinguishing between those with physical disabilities and moderate learning or behavioural problems, and those who have severe emotional, behavioural and social problems (now called EBSD) ...

The Special Educational Needs and Disability Act 2001 has strengthened the right of these children to be educated at a mainstream school. However, many young people with severe forms of EBSD [Emotional Behavioural and Social Deficit] need alternative provision.

If the Government's commitment to 'personalized education' is to mean anything, every child must have an education appropriate to his or her needs. And if they simply can't cope with mainstream education, despite the best support, we must offer the right alternatives. Unless we do so, we not only fail them, we also fail their classmates whose chance to learn is constantly disrupted ... there are not enough long-term places for pupils with severe problems.

We now need extra specialist provision. Of course, effective provision is expensive. But earlier identification is already saving money by overcoming less severe special needs early on ...

We need new types of special school and more specialist units. This requires a new approach from ministers and teaching unions. The Government should promote and fund small special schools and units for those for whom mainstream is ineffective.

And the NASUWT should champion integration for those who would have been wrongly isolated in special schools in the past and who are succeeding in mainstream education.

Finally, a piece from the *Daily Mail* some 14 months later on 9 June 2005:

DISASTER OF 'INCLUSIVE' SPECIAL NEEDS TEACHING, BY THE WOMAN BEHIND IT

By Laura Clark, Education Reporter

The woman behind the drive to educate children with special needs in mainstream schools admitted yesterday it had been a disaster.

In an extraordinary climbdown, Baroness Warnock said she believed the system was failing thousands of vulnerable youngsters.

The 81-year-old academic said the inclusive approach had been a 'bright idea in the 1970s' but admitted it really isn't working.

The policy had resulted in a 'disastrous legacy' of forced removal of youngsters from special schools, she said.

The pressure to push them into mainstream education had created 'confusion of which the children are the casualties' ...

Her change of heart comes nearly 30 years after her landmark inquiry into special needs education spawned the current system.

Lady Warnock is a pillar of the liberal education establishment whose 1978 report declared that children with special educational needs must be taught with their peers wherever possible.

Her recommendations formed the basis of the 1981 Education Act which gave schools new responsibilities for accommodating such pupils...

According to the 1981 act, those with special educational needs have a 'learning difficulty, which may be the result of a physical or sensory disability, an emotional or behavioural problem or developmental delay'.

It also takes in those 'having a disability which prevents or hinders them from making use of educational facilities'. After coming into power in 1997, Labour speeded up the integration of special needs pupils with the closure of nearly 100 special schools ...

Teachers have complained the inclusion policy has resulted in disturbed youngsters wrecking lessons for thousands of pupils in mainstream schools ...

Lady Warnock, also an influential authority on medical ethics, has called for a fundamental rethink of special needs education.

'Governments must come to recognize that, even if inclusion is an ideal for society in general, it may not always be an ideal for school,' she wrote for the Philosophy of Education Society of Great Britain.

She said the approach 'springs from hearts in the right place' but said its implementation and the shifting of pupils out of special schools was a 'disastrous legacy'.

With this distinction Lady Warnock touches on the wider aspects of this whole question, namely our social attitude in general, as distinct from educational requirements and possibilities.

On the one hand, it is healthy for children to learn meeting others who are different, perhaps even strikingly so. It is the mark of a civilized society, after all, not only to tolerate and accept its less able citizens but to see it as their task to support them whenever possible. And it is healthy too for children to experience and respect adults who have developed such social awareness.

On the other hand this does not mean that all children could or should always be educated by the same methods, or even in the same classroom. Special skills need to be employed and special settings provided, at least for a time. Lady Warnock is emphatic on these needs. In her article she finally 'called for an independent committee to conduct a "radical review" of the current system and suggested strengthening the role of special schools'.

How was it possible then—taking into account Mary Warnock's measured attitude—that her name became associated with the idea of wholesale inclusion? The final article in our series appeared five months later (11 November 2005) in the *Times Educational Supplement* and may answer some of our questions. Very suitably it was entitled

THE CURIOUS CASE OF THE WARNOCK REPORT

It was a landmark for special needs but how independent were its findings? Asks Robin Jackson.

In her recent General Teaching Council for Scotland annual lecture 'From integration to inclusion', Mary Warnock provides some illuminating insights into the workings of the committee of inquiry into the education of children and young people, which she chaired. Of particular interest is her reference to the key role played by the secretariat of the Department of Education and Science in helping to shape the direction and content of the Warnock Report. According to Lady Warnock, the secretariat wrote the initial papers that formed the foundation of the committee's work, decided what research needed to be done, chose the schools that the committee members would visit and provided the questions that should be asked. One is left to wonder how independent this 'independent but government-financed committee' really was.

A curious omission in her lecture is any reference to the fact the Warnock committee had been forced to accept the case for integration well before the report was published. The last minute incorporation of clause 10 into the 1976 education bill changed the emphasis of education for handicapped children and young people from provision in special schools to provision in ordinary schools.

It is now accepted that clause 10 had been introduced as a result of pressure applied by a small, powerful and readily identifiable lobby which represented the interests of a minority within the 'handicapped' population ... The tactics employed by this lobby succeeded in outmanoeuvring the Government, the DES and most of the professional organizations. It was a pre-emptive strike taken by a lobby which had concluded that the Warnock committee might, at the end of its deliberations, not give unqualified support for a policy of integration.

The introduction of clause 10 into the 1976 bill caused an instant tidal wave of critical reaction. The National Association of Schoolteachers and Union of Women Teachers issued a statement citing difficulties in implementing the proposals. A letter from Lady Warnock was published in *The Times Educational Supplement* criticizing the inclusion of clause 10. A leader in the *Times* observed that the legislation would lead to considerable controversy. Later, the *Times* carried a letter from Lady Warnock repeating her concern that the clause had been passed precipitately.

The National Union of Teachers made it clear that the inclusion of clause 10 was quite unexpected since it legislated for the provision of special education in ordinary schools in advance of the findings of the Warnock committee. Serious doubts were also expressed as to the effects of implementing such a clause.

In the NUT's view, this could not be seen as progress but rather a decline in the provision of special education, and a subsequent deterioration of educational opportunities for children with disabilities. Reference was also made to the fact that the NUT had submitted evidence to the Warnock committee warning it against approving a policy of integration ...

The lack of commissioned research inevitably meant that the committee became unduly reliant on the less than objective evidence submitted by pressure groups.

The claim made in the editorial introduction to the impact pamphlet that the Warnock committee was responsible for pioneering an 'integrative' or 'inclusive' approach needs to be treated with caution. For, as the Warnock Report itself acknowledged, it was section 10 of the 1976 Education Act, later to be incorporated into the 1981 Education Act, that shifted the emphasis on special educational provision in the direction of greater integration in ordinary schools.

In those circumstances the Warnock committee can scarcely be characterized as pioneering when it was in fact having to follow— and one suspects reluctantly—a path that had already been created.

Robin Jackson is a professional development consultant.

While in this first 'theme' a more external framework is given of the Peredur work, against the backdrop of the special educational situation in the country as a whole, the following 'Themes' should convey more of the substance in the life and work of Peredur Home School. It enabled many children and young people to progress into their future lives with a measure of purpose and independence.

6. The Environment—Obstacle or Opportunity?

The word 'environment' has made headlines only in recent decades. As a serious subject, care for the environment has now become of worldwide concern. However, the individual may often feel rather helpless when faced with its enormity. But as to environment on a small scale, for instance in the upbringing and education of small children, just about *everything* in their environment plays a vital role in their development. Even in later years of growth what has been 'home' can go on playing a vital role. But what if that has been lacking? Can we make up for it later? We must try! Quite typical is the book title which David Wills—that pioneer in social work with adolescents—gave to one of his later writings, *A Place Like Home*. I met David quite frequently in the gatherings of our Association of Workers for Maladjusted Children (AWMC). In his report of a summer conference, which had been held at the Peredur Home School, he rather charmingly referred to the mood that can be created: 'During the weekend the Peredur bees were swarming. And something of the sweetness of honey seemed to pervade the place as a whole.'

What meets the eye, what pleases the ear, what tickles the palate—in short, what can delight the senses—can spell 'home' in the widest sense, especially if that is linked with the rhythms of time, such as the seasons of the year. One such attempt can even be the exterior and the interior of the buildings we erect. What follows is the detailed description of one of Peredur's efforts at producing 'a place like home' in the widest sense.

★　　　★　　　★

Just before we enter into that, here comes the surprise of a letter from an early student-helper, as unexpected for the reader as it was for me! I let it speak for itself.

Dear Siegfried,

A very long time has passed since the year I spent at Peredur. It has been one of the very important years in my life. It made me decide to become a teacher. Although over 40 years have passed it is still so present in my mind and heart, the time we had together ... As Cornwall is a part of my life and as there is the strong desire to meet you again to talk about so many things we have gone through and are looking forward to, I want to ask you if it is possible to meet again ...

Of course I wrote a welcoming reply that we will make it possible! Now back to the early development.

Building a school house?

A serious need in the early years of the Peredur Home School was that of new classrooms. What we had to begin with, a five-bedroom house with five servants' quarters on the third floor, was adequate for a small group of children. But as their number grew we had to create more classroom space. The first and easiest solution on offer was to buy disused army huts which were readily available at that time. At one end of the scale stood this immediate and 'practical' proposal. At the other end we saw the challenge of taking the bull by the horns, which was to look at this need as a welcome challenge to build something that could support our educational efforts in a way that would speak for itself, with which the children would be able to identify and which could even, through its forms and colours, have a healing effect. This latter alternative won the day.

The planning of a new school building

The late Kenneth Bayes, FRIBA, an experienced London architect, who was interested in Rudolf Steiner's architectural work, was willing to undertake a new organic design. However, he had had no previous experience of that. To support his preparatory studies Joan and Siegfried Rudel made a point of visiting the first ever Waldorf School in Germany from where they brought back a number of photographs of the recently rebuilt, artistically designed School House in Stuttgart.

Our new school building at East Grinstead was eventually designed as two wings linked by a central entrance hall. This was done also in order to disperse the noise (for which same reason the passages were planned to be extra wide). This 'two-wing' design also made it possible to divide the whole building programme into two successive stages. The wing nearest to the existing cottage was to be built first and would have to stand by itself (while already in full use, of course), with a provisional blocking-off of its passage at the far end which later would lead into the main entrance hall and from there into the second wing—the latter was to be built at about 130° to the first. The first building phase was carried out in the years 1955-56. The second wing was scheduled to be built as soon as it would become financially possible. In fact the building of it began in 1958. It will be appreciated that the beautiful but unfinished first wing by itself helped to raise further funds to complete the building as a whole.

However, before going into the details and working functions of the two wings it would seem appropriate at this point to briefly describe the special act of the laying of the foundation stone which, of course, preceded any of the visible building activity.

The laying of the foundation stone

The actual laying of the Foundation Stone in 1955 was a special ritual conceived and conducted by Francis Edmunds, then a teacher at Michael Hall School and an early Trustee of Peredur Home School and who later founded Emerson College. A large number of Waldorf teachers who were congregated for a Michael Hall School conference in nearby Forest Row came to join in the occasion. All people present, as part of the ceremony, signed their names on a parchment scroll which was placed in a copper pentagon-dodecahedron. To it were added samples of the seven planetary metals, each brought forward by one of the Peredur school-children who spoke suitably chosen words as they handed them over. The final 'gift' before the foundation stone was lowered into the ground was a special verse by Rudolf Steiner which links education with the task of healing. This had first been spoken by Dr Kirchner-Bockholt (who later became the head of the Medical Section at the Goetheanum) when she had attended the official opening of the Peredur Home School on 2 February 1952.

The functions of the two school house wings

The first wing was conceived as serving a dual purpose, in itself not an artistic feature. However, it fulfilled two different functions, at different times, in a satisfactory way. This was due both to the excellent architectural planning as well as the expert building skills of James Waters & Sons of Forest Row. The way it worked is as follows. Two large folding/sliding doors enabled the division of the whole space to be used as three separate rooms, namely two main-lesson classrooms at each end and a handwork room in the middle. On special occasions these dividing doors could be folded to the sides and the whole space, or two thirds of it as the case might be, could then be used for concerts, performances or the Sunday services. A removable stage of boxes and side stairs was constructed for use at the east end.

Now followed a two-year pause for saving and raising more money, and then two further years of building the entrance hall and the second wing—at about 130° to the first. The fall of the land, towards the far end of this new wing, facilitated a split-level arrangement as follows: a teachers' room and weaving room upstairs, woodwork room and cloakrooms downstairs, with the last-minute addition of a chemistry laboratory in a basement.

Because of the two-phase building programme, the foundation stone had remained in open ground for altogether four years until its position could now finally be marked indoors in a permanent way, namely in the middle of the entrance hall, as originally planned. This position is signified, up to the present day, by the bronze plaque let into the wooden floor, with an inscribed pentagon-dodecahedron.

The two murals and the name Peredur

It will have become clear from the foregoing that it had been the main aim from the beginning to give the entrance hall a special character. In a way it was to become, and did become, the central point or focus of the whole building. Its main entrance was used only on festive occasions, and the inner space was to convey something of the ethos of the whole place. Two special features were to assist in this and both were to be newly created works of art. The sculptor John Wilkes responded to our request to create a sculpted head of Rudolf Steiner and this was given its place on a special ledge that was built for it on the inner wall of the entrance hall where the two wings are joined. It is unfortunate that, a few years later, it fell from its position in a dramatic accident and was destroyed beyond repair.

Two even more prominent artistic features relate to the name 'Peredur', which had been suggested for the school by Violet Plinke, the anthroposophical scholar of history and literature. Two murals were commissioned to be carried out by Liane Collot d'Herbois. She chose two characteristic motives from the Parzival story ('Peredur' is that same character in the Welsh Mabinogion).

But why was the name 'Peredur' chosen for the new Home School in the first place? This has already been touched upon earlier and was also to be a challenge for the pupils. The children to be cared for and educated had to be helped over a difficult phase in their earlier years. 'Maladjusted'—a term no longer used now—was considered the only one out of a number of handicaps listed in the Government report *The Education of Maladjusted Children* (HMSO, 1955) which children had a chance of outgrowing during their childhood and/or later years. (We will return to this report in the chapter about 'Rhythm'.) It was felt by the Peredur founders that the children's own courage and strength of will would be needed and that the Parzival biography could be a powerful inspiration for them. Joan Rudel later also wrote a Peredur play which was performed by successive groups of children and whose inner participation was moving to watch.

This raises the question of how real, or even how justified, it is for the other enterprises who are now using these buildings simply to adopt the same name again.

Returning to the murals, it can not be assumed that the themes of the two murals are familiar to the reader. The first of the murals, on the right side upon entering through the main door and more in blue tones, shows Peredur (Parzival) as an unknowing youth asking his way to the Grail Castle—from which he is later banished after failing to ask the needful question. The second mural, on the left and more in golden tones, shows him when after many trials and tribulations he returns to the ailing king carrying the spear that had been lost through Amfortas' tragic failing. '*Den heil'gen Speer, ich bring ihn euch zurück*' (The holy spear, I bring it back to you!) as Richard Wagner's music-drama *Parsifal* has it. You can see in the background his mother Herzeleide who died when the youth suddenly left her and who now accompanies him like a guardian angel.

As to the actual creation of the murals, the following can be said. It was in the early sixties that Liane Collot d'Herbois painted them in what appears to be the historical fresco style, by transferring the whole picture, done on a life-sized board, section by section, each about four square feet, onto the actual walls. These small sections had to be prepared afresh every morning, one per day, with a special lime and plaster mixture. At least this is how the present writer remembers the procedure as he had to assist in the preparations, helping to make sure that only enough material was mixed every morning as would not dry out prematurely. It is remarkable how well the strength and radiance of most of the colours have lasted all these years.

It is to be hoped that these unique murals will be taken care of for further years.

The opening of the school building

Returning to the historical sequence of events, it was on St George's day, 23 April 1960, that the official opening of the new school building took place. On this occasion it was a conference for Steiner Education for

Special Needs that was taking place at the time and which added to the assembled company. The Deputy Director of Education of Surrey County Council gave the opening speech emphasizing that it was always the spiritual motivation that had given rise to a special building which would remain with it and determine its future. The architect Kenneth Bayes passed on the thanks he received to Mr King of James Waters & Son of Forest Row who then handed over the key of the new building to Joan and Siegfried Rudel as the Principals of the school. As he did so he declined the praise of his building skills which had been expressed, saying that it was always the will of the patrons which was the essential factor in making a new building possible. This seemed to include the good will of the assembled company, which was like an echo of the support given by those who had taken part in the earlier ceremony of the foundation stone laying five years previously.

Present on this occasion of the opening was also the artist Arne Klingborg, co-director of the anthroposophical centre in Järna (Sweden). He had already partaken in the final building stage of the second wing of the school building by painting the walls—and also taught others to paint them—by means of his new method of radiant translucent colouring now known as lazure painting.

While the opening of the school building had been the end of that particular building period it was at the same time the beginning of a new era. This was helped through the many years of continuing help, inspiration and cooperation which the Peredur enterprise received from Arne Klingborg in the decades that followed.

The bakery and granary

The idea of building a bakery had first arisen through the needs of one of the Peredur pupils whose future at 16 years of age seemed uncertain. Baking bread had been the only skill he had mastered, but that with enthusiasm. His father had offered to give a loan to the newly founded second company, the Peredur Farm and Craft Centre, so that a bakery could be built. Peredur had by then been able to enlarge its farming activities and to grow its own wheat. It should be said at this point that the development of work on the land in varied ways and the experience of the changing year with its seasonal festivals was becoming an ever-growing part of the educational scene. More of this in further chapters.

To make the new bakery more effective, the charity's maintenance man suggested the building of a large granary above the bakery which

In the Peredur bakery

could also house the Huby mill which had been designed by Maurice Wood, a biodynamic farmer and miller in Yorkshire. This did indeed enable the newly milled flour to come through a shaft straight into a flour bin in the bakery below. Kenneth Bayes had begun to work on the design and Arne Klingborg joined him in the final stages. Two wood-fired ovens were built, each capable of taking about 40 loaves. The design for these ovens had proved its worth in earlier years at the Sunfield Children's Homes, the first anthroposophical establishment for children with special needs in this country. (That is where Joan Rudel had first experienced the coming together of curative education with arts and practical skills.) The adjoining single-storey tract of the bakery building was for further practical purposes, such as a leather workshop, a yoghurt-making facility and a garage and maintenance section. This was also the time when a daily van round could be established which, in cooperation with other bio-dynamic farms, supplied people in the neighbourhood with bread, milk, yoghurt and vegetables in season.

The Homestead

This new building was to provide accommodation for more school children. Originally it should have been built higher up and further south-eastwards in order to be directly accessible from West Hoathly Road, but planning consent had not been granted. The changing level on the edge of the woodland, where the Homestead was eventually built, was not seen as an obstacle but was even welcomed by Arne Klingborg. He made good use of it by first of all planning on the higher level a large living room with a wider, gently curving bay window to the south-east, and then on the lower level both the dining room and kitchen with a wide open stairway between them. The two of them could thus be used as one large space on special occasions—such as wedding parties! Staff and children's rooms were also built on both levels further along to the south as well as upstairs. This house proved, in the way it had been built, to be very popular with both children and staff. It should be noted that the total number of children had risen by then to 60.

Jack Pye, benefactor and later Peredur trustee

The building of the Homestead had been made possible through a generous donation by Jack Pye, the successful builder who had worked his way 'up the ladder' and had vested his eventual fortune in the Jack and Mary Pye Trust in order to aid aspiring young people to establish themselves in life. He had just saved the Soil Association's Haughley Experiment from collapse by an injection of £40,000. He now willingly helped the Peredur Farm and Craft Centre with a loan to purchase the neighbouring Boyles Farm when it came up for sale in 1968 (170 acres). This enabled the Centre to farm on a larger scale and also to use the seventeenth-century farmhouse as another school leavers' hostel.

The Hostel for school leavers

As already mentioned in Chapter 5 on 'Special Schools', it was in the early sixties of the last century that the need of some form of support for 'maladjusted' school *leavers* was much spoken about in educational circles. 'A bridge into life' would be needed for young people of 16–18 years of age who had had the benefit of special education but were not quite ready to be independent. This need had also been much discussed in the Association of Workers for Maladjusted Children in which Peredur had been an active member ever since its inception. Joan and Siegfried Rudel had also been active in establishing a South-East Regional Branch of that Association.

After various official and private agencies had failed to come forward with any concrete proposals, we as the group of Trustees decided that the Peredur charity should initiate the new enterprise ourselves. On 5 May 1964, therefore, a public appeal for funds for building and equipping a hostel and workshops scheme was officially launched at which Professor Fulton, Vice-Chancellor of Brighton University, officiated. This appeal was promoted by a public relations officer and reached far and wide, especially through its well-produced appeal brochure. This had been written around a striking set of special photographs which had been skilfully chosen and arranged by Arne Klingborg.

The appeal succeeded in raising the scheduled £100,000, which made it possible for building to start almost immediately. This time Arne Klingborg, together with his colleague, the Scandinavian architect Erik Assmussen, designed the two-winged hostel at the northern end of the estate. Each wing could be relatively independent with separate sitting rooms and staff accommodation at each end, but sharing a central kitchen. The artistic design attracted much public attention and prompted a special opening. Since the building had a definitely Swedish character it became possible to invite Princess Margareta of Sweden (who lived in London

Joan with the princess of Sweden, 1967

and was married to an English businessman) to open the hostel, which was on 5 May 1966. Despite the heavy rain, it was a festive day. The Princess was charming as she looked around everywhere with great interest. She was certainly most surprised when, assembled in the school hall, all the children at a certain point burst into a well-known folk song sung in its original Swedish which had been especially rehearsed for the occasion! Arne Klingborg also gave a delightful talk about 'the impulse to build' as a truly human characteristic from early childhood onwards.

Two new training workshops

Concurrently with the hostel new specially designed workshops were built, also designed by Arne Klingborg and Erik Assmussen. It has to be said that this whole school leavers' scheme was meeting with much support and appreciation from the public and from bodies like the AWMC. This made it possible for school leavers from other special schools to be admitted to the Peredur training centre.

The workshop wing on the east side was angular in its overall shape and was designed to culminate visually in the high chimney for the central heating. (As an aside: the chimney was meant to be higher than it is now in order to give this tract a definite architectural focal point, but the builders made it shorter because 'it does not need to be higher', i.e. from a purely technical point!) This first building housed the pottery, with an entrance lobby and two workrooms—on the left for clay preparation and sculptural work and on the right for the gas-fired kiln and the preparatory glazing work. A very capable pottery instructor produced a lot of excellent wares and exhibited some of it at the Craftsmen's Potters Association in London. One of the students skilfully taught by her continues to do well in the Cornish Pottery of the Peredur Trust. The central space of this complex was for showroom facilities and for meeting with visitors, and the wider end-room became the enlarged shoe-repair and leather workshop.

What had not been able to be housed in this complex was a large weaving workshop and this was now given a lot of space in a separate large house with outer as well as inner staircases, facilities for dyeing wool downstairs and the actual weavery with all hand looms upstairs. This particular building was financed largely by a generous donation from Wates, the building firm. In appreciation of that it carried a special plaque by its front door for many years saying 'The Wates Weaving Shop' and the year it was built (1969). Wool from the Peredur flock of sheep was dyed and woven by our excellent weaving tutor into beautifully coloured material for dressmaking and smaller items like mats and cushion covers. Some of her students became very skilled indeed.

The idea of a move to Cornwall

The question may be asked: Why contemplate such a move while all this promising development was even now still incomplete? The reasons were threefold and have already been touched upon. The changes in the immediate environment were the most obvious factor—that is, the growing urbanization of the whole East Grinstead area, such as new housing developments, increase of traffic, the effect of the growth of Gatwick Airport and the continuing threat of an East Grinstead by-pass. The onset of the actual building of a by-pass road had been successfully delayed by a public campaign spearheaded by Peredur in alliance with a local Housing Association for three long years, 1971–74. The preferred route would have gone through seven fields of the Peredur farm. Eventually, when in 1974 East Grinstead became part of *West* Sussex, that County Council no longer made this road scheme a part of their immediate planning proposals!

The second motive sprang from the need to build up a new setting which would be no longer part of the school, in order to meet the needs of a group of young adults who had now outgrown even the school leavers scheme but still needed further support.

Finally, national policy was changing as far as the educational provision for children and adolescents with specials needs was concerned. The so-called Warnock Report (1975) had, as described in the previous chapter, recommended their integration into mainstream schools and this new idea had been incorporated into the next Education Act.

With all this in mind, the plans for the Peredur Trust to build a second school leavers' hostel and a hall were all shelved. Instead a move to the south-west of England was actively considered where a suitable, more rural setting would have to be found.

The actual move

The move of the whole Peredur enterprise was carried through in four main stages. In 1975, Basill Manor, near Launceston, north Cornwall came up for sale and seemed an ideal base for the development of an adult working community. A trust who had visited the Peredur work in Sussex

Basill Manor

now bought Basill Manor for this new impulse to take root. In 1978 the larger part of the Sussex farm, 180 acres, was sold and Tregillis Farm in Cornwall bought with the proceeds. In 1979, the main house and cottage and wider parts of the original Millfield estate were sold to the London School of Eurythmy. This enabled the Peredur Trust to acquire the Trebullom estate, in Cornwall, for school leavers in need of further support. This is most suitably situated halfway between Basill Manor and Tregillis Farm. In 1981, the school leavers' hostel in East Grinstead and its environs were sold to the Tobias School of Art and Therapy. Now the group of youngsters could move from the school leavers' compound of East Grinstead buildings to the new Trebullom estate in Cornwall. Our Trust was now caring for people aged 16 and over.

The new needs were thus met in quite a surprisingly short space of time, with the three new Cornish estates situated within a few miles of each other, and each developing in their special way and yet inter-connected.

We stood before a new situation, having lived and worked in houses of modern style, whereas those which were to become 'home' to us now had been built centuries ago. And yet, as Arne Klingborg eventually came to feel, they were of a 'timeless' architecture. The gardens and farms, too, were a new challenge for us. The Cornish soil of deep-lying granite and layers of 'shillets' of slate contrast now with the limestone and clay that widely underlay our Sussex soil. It poses a task that is still with us. And what of the wild and stormy elements now all around us? They may well call for a counterbalance indoors. Can that be through more art and music in the home? The history of Cornwall provides us with encouraging examples.

7. Nutrition—Help or Hindrance?

Here we have another subject, like Education, which is being discussed and written about a good deal, and this one by an even wider range of people. Nutrition, after all, is of some concern to everyone. I will begin more with 'hindrance' and end up more with 'help'.

There can be no question, of course, of attempting an overview of the whole field of literature on nutrition which, in any case, is being added to all the time. However, there are five authors whom I came across which impressed me by their competence of research and by their concern for the health of the nation in general. I have marked them simply as a) to e):

a) The first book that came to my notice is *Not All in the Mind* by Richard Mackarness, MB, BS, DPM, published in 1976 and going through its tenth printing in 1980. Even before acknowledging that 'this book has taken me seventeen years to write' the author places his motto thus: ' "Surely the time has come to put away the notion that psychiatry deals just with mind disease ... Only in Wonderland can we find the grin without the cat," by Foster Kennedy, Professor of Neurology, Cornell University as early as 1936.' In his first chapter already Dr Mackarness seems to have an inkling. Appreciating the help from his colleague he says, 'in the winter of 1958, Dr Ted Randolph had shown me several of his patients at the Swedish Covenant Hospital in Chicago. These cases persuaded me that food allergy might be the key to a number of stubborn, puzzling illnesses among patients in my general practice in England. Like most general practitioners, I had several patients crippled by illnesses for whose symptoms I was unable to find the cause.'

His further observations and wide-ranging conclusions are, therefore, the following:

A study of the lists of foods causing adverse reactions in Mrs A. and Michael B. suggests that possibly it is not always the foods themselves that are to blame, but their chemical contaminants. For example, Mrs A. could drink her own home-made soup, but soup from a tin upset her. Soup cans are often lined with a gold coloured resin to which some people are known to be sensitive. Also, many canned soup manufacturers add monosodium glutamate, a meaty-tasting flavouring agent which has recently come under fire in the *British Medical Journal* as causing the condition quaintly named Kwok's Quease or the Chinese Restaurant Syndrome.

Dr Robert Kwok is a research investigator practising in America who regularly eats Chinese food. One day, in a Chinese restaurant, he was suddenly seized with the most frightful griping pain in his chest, running up into his neck. He thought he was going to faint, and more or less collapsed across the table. The acute pain, which he thought was the beginning of a heart attack, subsided after a few minutes, but it left him shaken and determined to find out what had brought on such alarming symptoms. After much research with interested colleagues, he eventually came up with the answer: he had an allergy to monosodium glutamate, which some Chinese chefs add in considerable quantities to the food they prepare. Kwok first published his own case in the *New England Journal of Medicine* (1968).

At the end of my article reporting the cases of Mrs A. and Michael B., I suggested that allergy to foods and chemicals was a much more common cause of chronic ill-health than most doctors imagined. Here are the concluding paragraphs:

Conclusions

Many theories have been put forward to account for the increase in the number of patients with neurosis and psychosomatic illness today. The psychiatrists have persistently claimed that they have the secret, but somehow they have failed to give the GP a solution he can use.

I do not think we are being subjected to much more psychological stress now than we were twenty-five years ago, but I am sure that the sophistication and adulteration of food with chemical additives has increased enormously in that time and so has the consumption of processed starch and sugar (white bread, cakes, biscuits, sweets and soft drinks).

It would be surprising if people were *not* allergic to pesticides put into the ground and sprayed on crops, to flour 'improvers', anti-staling agents, emulsifying compounds, artificial colourings, preservatives and the whole terrifying array of potentially toxic substances now being added to our food in order to improve its appearance, flavour, shelf-life and profitability.

Why should psychosomatic or functional illness not be a manifestation of allergy to these new synthetic chemicals which we are eating

more and more as the supermarkets multiply? I believe the Stone Age
elimination diet to be a means not only of answering this question, but
also of giving relief to thousands of people whose health has been
affected in this way.

I have given a good deal of space to Dr Mackarness's book as it is no
longer in print.

b) Another researcher concentrated his work especially on the effect
which refined sugar can have on the human organism. He was Professor
John Yudkin, MD, PhD, FRCP, FRSC, FI Biol., who became Emeritus
Professor of Nutrition at London University. His book *Sweet and
Dangerous* was first published in the USA and in this country, later in the
same year, as *Pure, White and Deadly*.

> ... what little research there had been already showed that sugar in our
> diet might be involved in the production of several conditions,
> including not only tooth decay and overweight but also diabetes and
> heart disease.
>
> Since that time research has produced further evidence that sugar
> is implicated in these conditions, and has also added to the list of
> diseases in which the sugar we eat may possibly, or even probably,
> be a factor.

Fourteen years later a much enlarged edition was written and the
publishers (Penguin Viking) wrote:

> This extensively rewritten and expanded edition of *Pure, White and
> Deadly* reveals the new evidence that makes the book's title even more
> appropriate today. Professor Yudkin explains in everyday language his
> remarkable discoveries about sugar's drastic effects on the body, such as
> the increased development of dental caries, heart disease, diabetes and
> other conditions. He pays particular attention to the effects on children
> of high sugar consumption and shows how they, and everyone else, can
> benefit from cutting down their sugar intake. *Pure, White and Deadly*
> also asks why we know so little about the need to reduce our sugar
> consumption. The answer, according to Professor Yudkin, is the sugar
> industry itself, which has made strenuous efforts to dismiss the evidence
> against sugar and limit adverse publicity.

c) *Your Daily Food*, by Doris Grant (Faber & Faber), which unfortunately is now out of print. The author concentrates on the effect of
white bread.

In June 1971, one of the strongest warnings yet to appear regarding the dangers of chemicals in our food was published in a Swiss scientific journal, *Experientia*. It is of special significance, and comprises a statement, 'Pro Natura Integra', signed by a team of internationally renowned scientists. This team included two Nobel prizewinners in medicine, the assistant editor of the *British Medical Journal*, the President of the French Medical Society, the retiring head of the Pasteur Institute, and Sir Julian Huxley, the first Director General of the United Nations Education Scientific and Cultural Organization. These scientists warned that the effect of environmental pollution on the human organism together with the iatrogenic diseases caused by modern drugs and the diseases of civilization 'are among the monumental issues of our day'.

This team of scientists also warned that many of the compounds being consumed today are not related to combating disease but to making things easy for us; they are in demand for our physical comfort and economic enrichment. 'Society,' they affirm, 'has reached a stage of development where the stresses and strains produced by its own speed of technological advance are not only overtaking man's power of adaptability—both physical and mental—but are endangering his very survival.' These scientists point out, however, that whereas the cost of halting environmental pollution would be astronomical the cost of preventing further *internal* pollution is within our economic means and perfectly feasible if this problem is tackled *now*.

Subsequently Doris Grant draws our attention to the problems of white bread in particular.

The champions of white bread overlook the fact that the removal of the greater parts of eight vitamins and of twelve minerals from the flour *distorts* the natural balance of these nutrients and that the quite inadequate restoration of the four statutory additives (B_1, niacin, iron and chalk) may only compound this distortion. Biochemical research is now showing that the amount of a nutrient in a food is not nearly so important as its quantitative relationship to other nutrients—the ratio, in other words, of one to another. In white flour, for instance, there is twice the amount of potassium in relation to magnesium as compared with wholewheat flour. In *Soil, Grass and Cancer*, André Voisin draws attention to the disadvantages of this increase and the possible consequences with regard to cancer and thrombosis ... Another factor overlooked by the champions of white bread, and one which is of great significance, is the removal of the bran, *one of the great advantages of wholewheat bread*. Apart from the fact that it is a key source of the B vitamins and that it supplies linolenic acid which helps to prevent coronary heart disease, its main importance lies in the necessary roughage, or fibre, which it provides ... Yet another overlooked factor in white bread is the extra amount, compared to wholewheat bread, which must be eaten in order to satisfy the hidden hunger produced by its unsatisfying effect. No wonder obesity is now a serious problem at all ages. It should now be plainly obvious that anyone who claims today that there is no nutritional difference between white bread and wholewheat bread just hasn't done his homework!

... Not content with robbing the flour of the greater part of some of its nutrients, the modern flour miller proceeds, literally, to send this flour to the gas chamber! In *Star & Furrow*, Mrs Joan Rudel, of the famous Peredur School for maladjusted children, has described a visit to this gas chamber during a tour of a modern mill. At the end of the tour, having seen the milling process and, lying about the floor, the mystery sacks whose contents the miller would not divulge, she and her friends [I was one of them! SWR] were taken to see the gas chamber where the flour is 'gassed' to speed up the ageing process and to bleach it: before entering the chamber they were warned to remove their macs 'in case they were affected'. The gassing apparatus was behind locked doors and tubes led from these to the bleaching chamber. 'As far as could be perceived,' comments Mrs Rudel, 'no gas was escaping from the still, but after a few moments we were told to go out, as the fumes were so dangerous if inhaled. It is interesting to speculate what effect this gas might have when the flour so treated reaches the digestive system.' Not surprisingly, at Peredur they not only bake excellent bread in brick ovens heated in the old-fashioned way, but they mill their own flour from grain grown without poisonous dressings or artificial fertilizers.

The following anecdote from the life at the Peredur Home School, not without relation to the foregoing. A fair-haired, lively pupil came to us as a difficult to manage youngster—and that he was indeed, overactive to put it mildly! Over time he had begun to become more peaceful in himself and sleeping better at night when his parents came for advice regarding his behaviour in the holidays. The first week or so was usually quite all right, they said, but then the old pattern of restless, overactive behaviour would come back again, unbearably so. Could it be, they asked, that it had something to do with nutrition? They had heard that ours was a wholefood diet, theirs was not and much of it was left to the youngster's own choices. Should they also adopt a wholefood way? We encouraged them to try that and it worked! The boy gradually learnt to maintain his more balanced behaviour throughout his holidays, and also his deeper sleep at night, much to the relief of his parents.

This episode illustrates some of the everyday work that can be done in practical life.

d) The next two books are still available in print and will, therefore, be dealt with only briefly. The first of them is by Maria Geuter and entitled *Herbs in Nutrition*—a very remarkable and wide-reaching book! Although first published as long ago as 1962, it is now again available, this time produced by the American Bio-Dynamic Publishers. It can be ordered through the Bio-Dynamic Agricultural Association.[1] I knew Maria Geuter. She was a very modest and retiring person and I remember from our visiting her in her later years that Joan urged her to put her special cooking skill also into a printed book. We were sorry that she never did it—but someone else has done it now!

e) This is Wendy Cook, the second one to come to 'help'. Her book was published in 2006 and was reprinted already in 2007. *The Biodynamic Food*

In the greenhouse attending lettuces, Trebullum

and Cookbook it is called, and the subtitle reads: 'Real nutrition that doesn't cost the earth'. The opening chapters have telling titles:

1. The Culture of Food and Cooking through the Ages
2. The Ethics of Modern Food Culture
3. What is Biodynamic Farming?

The larger of the two sections, which contains the recipes, has seasonal chapters as well as catering for a variety of people and occasions. However, I would warmly encourage the reader to study Part 1 first, modestly called 'Background', however soon he or she would wish to get to the colourful recipe section! It is rare to find a practical book that looks nice, is pleasant to read, can teach the reader, and which also gives a philosophical opening to the ethos of the whole. A hopeful ending to this narrative!

Note
1. Painswick Inn Project, Gloucester Street, Stroud, Glos, GL5 1QG.

8. 'For the Rhythm of Life is a Powerful Beat'

Our motto for this chapter is taken from the 1969 musical *Sweet Charity*, with its lyrics by Dorothy Fields. She leads up to it as follows:

When I started down the street last Sunday,
Feelin' mighty low and kind o' mean,
Suddenly a voice said, 'Go forth, neighbour!
Spread the picture on a wider screen!'

And the voice said, 'Neighbour, there's a million reasons
Why you should be glad in all four seasons!
Hit the road, neighbour,
Leave your worries and strife!
Spread the religion of the rhythm of life.'

For the rhythm of life is a powerful beat,
Puts a tingle in your fingers and a tingle in your feet!
Rhythm on the inside, rhythm on the street,
And the rhythm of life is a powerful beat!

What rhythms strike us right away when we hear such a song, or just listen to the words? First of all, surely, the rhythm of our own breathing. It mirrors the life of the soul. From the extreme of anxious suspense or fear—an intense inbreathing—it can swing just as strongly to a welcome relief in the breathing out. The pendulum of the soul can swing to and fro in a variety of ways. We always hope—do we not?—that a healthy rhythm will prevail. At stressful times, the longer rhythm of a blissful night and a day of new resolve may come into its own; so may even that of the week, with a deliberate acceptance throughout the week of outer demands to be relieved at the weekend by the blessing of inner recovery. To crown it all, the rhythm of the year with its ever-changing seasons can always strike us afresh if we can but allow ourselves to enter into their magic. We might indeed be helping then to 'spread the religion of the rhythm of life'.

Through making Peredur a Home School we were able to make various yearly rhythms into real supports. Christmas stands out in particular. Here is an article Joan Rudel had been asked to write for the *Weleda News* (Winter 1964):

Christmas in a Rudolf Steiner Home-School
Joan Rudel, BA

People look East. The time is near
Of the crowning of the year.
Make your house fair as you are able,
Trim the hearth and set the table.

The beautiful carol rings out in the frosty air while the eastern sky begins to glow with the winter sunrise. It is the first Sunday of Advent, and a small group of teachers and housemothers go from house to house waking the children with an Advent song. After singing outside, they go into each house, and all the children come crowding down the stairs to see the first candle alight on the wreath of green fir hanging in the living room.

At Peredur Home School and many other Rudolf Steiner Homes and Schools this is the beginning of Christmas—or nearly the beginning. Perhaps for the children the very first exciting realization of the nearness of Christmas came a few days earlier when everyone was sitting together in the hall, grown-ups and children, too, singing carols and weaving the sweet smelling fir branches into Advent wreaths large and small for the various dwelling-houses and classrooms. Next Sunday there will be two candles burning on each wreath, then three, until on the last Sunday before Christmas four candles are lit.

At breakfast on Advent Sundays a candle with a sprig of fir in a red apple burns in front of each place, and the candle flames flutter in the buzz of many cheerful voices. Some children gaze in wonder at the dozens of candle flames; others push the fir twigs into the flame to see the sparks and smell the pungent scent. At supper, after music and a story, again in the light of many candles, they will eat the apples. The burned-down candles tell them that the first day of Advent is over, and that they have travelled one day along the path leading to Christmas, the crown of the year. Every day now they will sing a verse of the Advent carol in the morning at breakfast and know by counting the candles that are lit on the wreath how much further they have gone along that path.

By 24 December most of the children have gone home, after seeing the two old peasant Oberufer plays of the story of Adam and Eve, and then the Nativity of Jesus, performed by their teachers. But some always remain because they cannot go home, or because they have chosen to stay. Christmas Eve is a quiet day. The Advent wreaths,

Lyres being played under the Christmas tree for a circle of listening children

which have lost their fresh green during the weeks they have hung indoors, disappear. During the day, new fir branches and holly too are brought in to decorate the house. In the early evening, the children, in their best clothes, come quietly on to the dark landing, waiting for that beautiful moment when they will go downstairs to the Christmas Tree.

At last the time comes. Singing, they go down and see the dark tree standing in a radiance of light. In a Rudolf Steiner School the Christmas Tree is not hung with the usual tinsel and coloured balls, nor even presents. Spread out over the branches are thirty white candles with three red ones on the topmost branch, and thirty-three red roses, which point to the thirty years of the life of Jesus Christ on earth and the three years of his ministry after the baptism in Jordan. There are other signs too, painted with gold, that tell of the history of man and the earth, the aeons of God-guided planetary evolution stretching from a remote past to a remote future, and the development of man himself towards an ever greater perfection, only made possible by the incarnation, death and resurrection of the Christ Himself. Sheltered beneath the lowest spreading branches is the Crib, the scene of the Nativity, laid out on a landscape of rocks, mosses and ferns. Under the lighted tree, on Christmas Eve, sounds out the beautiful melody of 'Es ist ein Ros entsprungen'[1] to the accompaniment of lyres and violins, and the children hear the story of the Birth as told by St Luke, before going in to their festive candlelit Christmas Eve supper.

Christmas Eve is a quiet, thoughtful and inwardly joyful celebration of the first Christmas with all that it means for men on earth.

On Christmas Day the note of jubilation becomes more outward. After taking part in the beautiful Children's Christmas Service written by Dr Steiner, everyone goes together to the school farm. This is a much loved excursion, and has its roots in old European Christmas custom and legend. First we visit the cows and calves and give them a special Christmas treat of fresh cabbages or apples; then to the horse, the sheep and the chickens. While walking over the fields in the winter sunshine and feeding the animals as they press closely around, delighted at the unusual throng of human beings and an extra bite, deep feelings arise in the children of gratitude and love for the wonderful world of nature. And after feeding the animals, who so much depend on man for their well-being, the children go to the present-room. There each child finds his own little table full of presents, which will give him pleasure for many days to come.

On Christmas afternoon, as on every afternoon until 6 January, there is music, singing and a story under the Christmas tree, and meals by candlelight at the long decorated table every day. It is almost as if, on 6 January, when the tree disappears and the flames of the last candles die down, one goes through a doorway leading from the warm, magical, shining realm of Christmastime into the ordinary everyday world. But in their hearts children and grown-ups too carry into the New Year the warmth and light of these wonderful Christmas experiences.

Here ends the account of a yearly rhythm. But shorter rhythms can be fostered as well. Thus weekends, throughout the year, lent themselves to lively Sunday afternoons with storytelling of adventures and heroism, or just good fun, and always interlaced with singing, music or posing riddles! These and similar rhythms lived on in the lasting memories of past pupils as we gather from letters which have reached us often after many years. The following message, which I received recently—for my birthday, much to my surprise—began thus:

It has been my immense good fortune and pleasure to have known you for the bulk of those 80 years, beginning with our first meeting in February 1952 as a prospective pupil for the newly established Peredur Home School in East Grinstead. Shortly thereafter, on 20 March 1952 to be precise, I began what were to be the most transformative four years of my life as a Peredur pupil. Those four years were all too short, but the seeds that had been sown and nurtured during that brief period are lasting me a lifetime.

However welcome then the varied rhythms can be in a special school, do they occur in the adult world of today? Even when they do, they can be grossly interfered with. Generally speaking, adults may try hard to cope with adult crises, of whatever length and nature—but what about the children then? They may find themselves confronted with an insecure or even turbulent world. The reader may have heard the answer to the question: What is a maladjusted child? 'A normal child reacting normally to a maladjusted environment.' One-sided as this answer may seem, it does point to one aspect of the problem. The other, of course, lies with the children as individuals. It is there that we tread on uncertain ground, at least to begin with.

The term 'maladjusted' has gone out of use now but it had not in 1950, when a Committee on Maladjusted Children was set up by the then Minister of Education, Mr George Tomlinson. I remember the good fortune of meeting three of its members—Dr Mildred Creak, Dr Alford and Mr Lumsden—at inspections and conferences. The Committee's Underwood report in 1955 contains many wise observations and I quote, to begin with, from its Introduction.

> Now that we have reached the end of our labours we feel bound to ask ourselves what we have achieved as a result of nearly five years' consideration of the problem referred to us. Those who may have expected from us a wholly novel insight into the nature of maladjustment or new and even revolutionary ideas about the way in which it should be treated will no doubt be disappointed with what we have to say. We do not even offer a tidy plan for dealing with the problem, nor have we been able to provide accurate estimates of its size.
>
> In our view it would not have been realistic to attempt anything as ambitious as this. Too little is yet known about maladjustment in children and the ways in which it can be successfully treated to make it possible to generalize or to suggest ready-made solutions; fifteen years ago the very term 'maladjustment' was not in common use.

Here we have a very modest assessment of their 'labours'. It is all the more worth reading. May I plead with the reader not to ignore this Report. It can have lasting value in our own time. The next section I recommend are the first six paragraphs of their 'Scope of the Enquiry'. The Committee clearly spans their grasp beyond childhood and adolescence to include adult life. Their other remarkable awareness is the twofoldness of mal-adjustment, as hinted at twice, however briefly, but clearly, in this section. (The emphasis will be mine—SWR.)

Already the two opening paragraphs hold words of wisdom.

A man can develop his powers to the full and lead a happy life only if he achieves some measure of adjustment or of harmony with those around him and with the circumstances in which he is placed. Not that he need be satisfied with his environment; some environments are so unhealthy that they ought to be altered. Without the characteristically human attitude of discontent with things as they are, there would be no development either of the individual or of the community, but it is possible to combine even a burning determination to right wrongs with mental balance and tranquillity of disposition. Adjustment how-ever can never be complete; continual adjustment and readjustment are necessary throughout life.

Fortunately, most people remain reasonably adjusted to their environment and manage their lives well enough. Those who fail to achieve any real adjustment do not necessarily have domestic differ-ences or come in conflict with the law nor, in the case of children, are they necessarily unruly. **Indeed, some of those who are most severely maladjusted are quiet and passive.**

Moreover, maladjustment is not the same as unconventionality or oddness of behaviour or belief, which may not do a person or his fellows any harm. As Sterne pointed out in *Tristram Shandy*, 'have not the wisest men in all ages . . . had their hobby-horses; . . . and so long as a man rides his hobby-horse peaceably and quietly along the King's highway, and neither compels you or me to get up behind him—pray Sir, what have either you or I to do with it?' A man's idiosyncrasies may even be a sign of self-confidence and strength, and lend attractiveness to his character.

Nor can maladjustment be equated with educational backwardness or mental dullness. It may affect people in the whole range of intelli-gence.

What is characteristic of those who do not achieve any real adjust-ment with their environment is that they are insecure and unhappy, even though this may be concealed by a mask of self-assurance; they tend to get on badly in their personal relationships, with father and mother, brothers and sisters, husband or wife, or their own children; and they may have failed to come to terms with their work.

Maladjustment is a term first used in the 1920s and only widely adopted, in this country at least, since the Second World War. The reality behind it has existed throughout history, but it is only during recent years that the serious implications of the problem have been realized. Its worst effects are seen in mental hospitals, divorce courts, and prisons, since **the close connection of maladjustment with disharmony in the home, delinquency and, above all, mental illness, cannot be doubted**.

The theme of maladjustment as an imbalance between two extremes will meet us again in the Music chapter.

Before concluding my review of this 'Report' I would like to insert a telling anecdote. It was during a large London meeting chaired by Dr Creak. A question was put forward by a member of the audience with some urgency: 'Why are there not more child guidance clinics and more psychiatric social workers?' Dr Creak replied, gently but firmly, that she did not think that this was the foremost question to ask. What she thought we should ask ourselves in the first place was—and she spoke with deep concern—'Why is it that there are a growing number of maladjusted children?'

It was therefore understandable that the Report under review, significantly enough, also had a section on education in the early years. Here, as a sample, is the opening paragraph of the chapter 'Development and Maturity'.

Education is deeply concerned with the process of maturing: indeed, it is in essence the means by which the immature are enabled to become mature. In this sense it takes place not only at school; **the whole environment, both human and material, in which the child grows up is the true educative medium**. Modern research suggests that the most formative influences are those which the child experiences before he comes to school at all, and that certain attitudes have then taken shape which may affect decisively the whole of his subsequent development.

Readers who have some acquaintance with Rudolf Steiner Education will feel on common ground here. Rudolf Steiner's early booklet *The Education of the Child* is often the trail-blazer for new Waldorf Schools, now grown in number to a worldwide movement of over a thousand schools. The element of rhythm plays a very important role, on many levels.

Returning one last time to the Underwood Report, we find the following short paragraph concluding the main chapter called 'The Nature, Symptoms and Causes of Maladjustment'. This paragraph is set apart from the main body of Chapter IV and stands by itself, to raise a fundamental question.

> ... it is not suggested that the causal factors we have mentioned inevitably produce maladjustment whenever they operate strongly. All are likely to have an effect on personality and all seem to be sufficiently clearly associated with maladjustment to be regarded as causes of it, but only some of the children affected by them become maladjusted to any significant degree. **The reasons why one child succumbs rather than another seem to be deep and, at present, obscure.**

This final sentence is actually a question and a very fundamental one at that. It is calling for an answer. Is there in human development a third influence, besides heredity and environment? One that can stand independently beside, or even above, the other two?

I recall in my own life having this very question rise up in my mind when I was 16 years old. I still remember where I was standing, with my father, by a bridge, and asking him. He was confirming it to me: 'Yes there is an essential being in everyone, each with his own destiny. Heredity and environment play a part, but not the only one.'

Very young children will sometimes call themselves, to begin with, by a self-made name, but only for a relatively short period of time. Then, at about the third year stage, they may begin to say 'I' when referring to themselves. Is that a premonition of his or her prophetically establishing their existence as an 'in-dividual' and with that an awareness of having descended from a higher sphere, the greatest rhythm of all? William Wordsworth has it in his *Intimations of Immortality From Recollections of Early Childhood*.

I

There was a time when meadow, grove, and stream,
The earth, and every common sight,
To me did seem
Apparelled in celestial light,
The glory and the freshness of a dream.
It is not now as it hath been of yore—
Turn whereso'er I may,
By night or day,
The things which I have seen I now can see no more.

II

The Rainbow comes and goes,
And lovely is the Rose,
The Moon doth with delight
Look round her when the heavens are bare,
Waters on a starry night
Are beautiful and fair;
The sunshine is a glorious birth;
But yet I know, where'er I go,
That there hath past away a glory from the earth ...

V

Our birth is but a sleep and a forgetting:
The Soul that rises with us, our life's Star,
Hath had elsewhere its setting,
And cometh from afar:
Not in entire forgetfulness,
And not in utter nakedness,
But trailing clouds of glory do we come
From God, who is our home:
Heaven lies about us in our infancy!
Shades of the prison-house begin to close
Upon the growing Boy,
But He beholds the light, and whence it flows,
He sees it in his joy;
The Youth, who daily farther from the east
Must travel, still is Nature's Priest,
And by the vision splendid
Is on his way attended;
At length the Man perceives it die away,
And fade into the light of common day.

Note

1. See *The Oxford Book of Carols* for the original German as well as for the English
   translation. Also see photograph of lyre playing under the Christmas tree.

9. Music, Art and Crafts—Pleasantries or More Than That?

Music

Shakespeare knows the magic of music. We hear it praised in *The Merchant of Venice*, Act V:

> None is so stockish, hard and full of rage,
> But music for the time does change his nature.
> The man who has not music in himself
> Nor is not moved with concord of sweet sounds,
> Is fit for treason, stratagem, and spoils;
> The motions of his spirit are dull as night
> And his affections dark as Erebus.
> Let no such one be trusted.

A German proverb echoes that message, in a somewhat homely fashion: 'Wo man singt, da lass dich ruhig nieder. Böse Menschen haben keine Lieder.' ('Where e'er they sing, go settle down with them. To sing is quite unknown to wicked men.')

Music is mysterious; everyone has their own individual experience of it. And yet it can bring with it a community-building element, and that in two different ways. One arises when we are listening to it quietly, that is, when music is played for us by others; the other experience, by way of contrast, is when we ourselves 'make' the music and can do so even without instruments when we *sing* and when the whole body can become an instrument. The one type of musical experience can have a quietening, soothing effect—it can engender an evening mood. The other, more lively type can be experienced as rousing and stimulating—more like a morning call.

Having studied Rudolf Steiner's educational lectures in our staff meetings, we came to be aware of two opposite tendencies in child development. We saw them often quite one-sidedly in maladjusted children: too fast, too slow; too early, too late; too hard, too soft. Could they not benefit from balancing activities, in either the one or the other direction? On the one hand, there were the overactive, ever-restless, even aggressive children who often found it hard to 'switch off' in the evenings.

Would they not benefit from an experience of peace through quietly *listening* to music at the end of the day? On the other hand, there were those who were always solitary, withdrawn and often, long after waking, still 'far away'. Would they not be helped into the day through an activity of lively *singing* and rhythmically moving in the mornings? To put it briefly, the motto would be 'peace in the evenings' for some and 'challenge in the mornings' for others. It was amazing how willingly the children accepted their special assignments!

There was a difference in the conduct of the two exercises. The evening session with the overactive children needed several staff to help in making sure that all settled down peacefully and remained thus, sometimes even by candlelight, so that the music could shed its blessing in peace. By way of contrast, the morning exercise was mostly conducted by just one experienced staff member who could, by example, inspire the morning activity, and transform the music into singing and rhythmical movement.

It was good to see how the children cooperated in these two contrasting activities. Perhaps it made them feel better by being more balanced for a while. By the way, not quite all the children took part; there were a few who did not clearly fall into either of the one-sidednesses—their problems were different.

The attentive reader will have noticed in the sections of the Underwood Report that were quoted in the preceding chapter on Rhythm that there, too, the two contrasting types of imbalance (or maladjustment) had been noted.

An earlier Peredur exercise, carried on for a time, had taken the form of music after bedtime, on the darkened landing, after settling for the night. I remember one evening when, during that time, we sat in the staff-room in conversation with the three government inspectors who had spent the first of two days with us. I had begged to leave our discussion at one point because it was, as I explained, the allotted time for the evening music to be played on the landing. 'Oh, can I come with you?' one of them asked. 'Of course,' I said, knowing he would have to sit on the stairs in the dark! But he did that quite happily whilst we played our lyre music by candlelight. On another such evening one little boy just would not settle down. So we let him come out—as a special treat!—to sit on the landing carpet and watch the players. When we had finished he did not get up: He had gone fast asleep and stayed like it even while we carried him back to bed! Before he left, one of the inspectors remarked, 'I noticed that throughout the day you have some quite definite moments of silence. That works like

Princess Margaretha of Sweden and pupils at Peredur, East Grinstead

magic. Seldom have I heard pedagogical insight expressed so spontaneously.'

With these descriptions we now leave our own musical efforts on one side and turn to a much larger one, though not directly connected with the life at Peredur. The reader may know the name of the German composer and conductor Bruno Walter, who was born in Berlin in 1876 and who died in San Francisco in 1962. I quote from a lecture he gave in Vienna in 1935 which will speak for itself. It could be called 'Music as a Magic Healer in Unexpected Quarters'.

About the Moral of Music

It was on a certain day in San Francisco that a man of middle age called on me—sadly I have forgotten the name of this remarkable philanthropist—and told me that he was a musician. Apart from that, and for quite a long time already, he had been taking an interest in the life of prisoners. While he had pondered about their destinies, their inner state of being and their possibilities for the future, he had come to the idea that it should be possible to reach their inner lives through music. He had succeeded in winning interest in his idea by the governor of a prison and had begun to instruct the prison inmates in part-singing. The result of his endeavours, carried on throughout several years, had been, as he explained, quite overwhelming: the behaviour of the prisoners changed fundamentally; not only that during the lessons their joy and their happiness shone forth. Also an astounding moderation occurred on the part of otherwise hardened and difficult men, both in their behaviour towards their superiors, as well as amongst each other. Instead of the usual punishments for any misdemeanours, it was only necessary now, in most cases, to use the threat of being excluded from the next choir practice in order to make the culprit conform.

As far as my visitor knew, no one discharged from the prison after his time of employment there, had returned to crime even though quite a number of years had gone by since then. If I remember correctly a change of prison governor had brought his work to a close. He now came to me, just as no doubt he went to many others, to interest me in his idea and to ask whether I would perhaps undertake to interest influential people in supporting his wish to take up his prison work again and altogether to encourage awareness of this whole idea.

My efforts, sadly, bore no fruit. But I believe that the philanthropist who had told me of his experiences in the prison was altogether on the right path.

The criminal has to be seen as an antisocial or at least asocial being, that is to say one who either hates society or just does not care. He takes from it what he wants to have by cunning or by force and that is his only relationship to it. He is, so to speak, alone in the world, locked up in his hardened ego and lives in a terrible solitude. Except in danger of imminent death no other opportunity was known to my informant when kind or admonishing words could penetrate the tough armour of this isolation or could win against the coarse and crude defence of the prisoner. What was denied to the word now succeeded with music: they sang in parts as a male-voice choir, finding new harmonies by themselves and sounding forth in their development by common effort. The one would sing B flat, the other D, the third F—they sang on and produced another concord. The lonely ones became 'socialized' through harmony, together producing something pleasant to hear by all as a group. They felt, deep down, the beauty of togetherness. We can understand that to be thus creating something beautiful together brought in its train the warmth of enthusiasm, even exaltation and the feeling of renewal.

I cannot recommend sufficiently strongly that such attempts should be taken up by us, too. Admittedly, their effect would be lost on the totally unmusical, but there are fewer of them that one thinks. Above all, I wish that part-singing were fostered more regularly in schools. Thus, already in children, a sense of community can be developed as it becomes manifest in harmonies.

I remember from my first years at school the bleakness engendered by our frequent singing in unison; and then the relief that choral singing gave me. I believe that it was not only the pleasure of the richer sound that I experienced but also the moral satisfaction through harmoniously entering into a closer connection with my fellow pupils . . .

In these last few observations a bridge is built to education.

Art

We cannot all be practising artists. But the uplifting element of Art as a visual experience can be experienced by all, both consciously and on a 'subliminal' level. It can also be practised and enjoyed in daily life, say in the way we dress or the way we lay the table for the next meal. But when especially gifted artists come our way, ready to transform our lives, do we always recognize their gifts and give them scope?

Throughout the many years of Peredur we have been fortunate on the many occasions when artists joined us. Eurythmy and painting in particular have always had a warm reception. But they have not yet again become an ongoing part and parcel of the life as they had been in Peredur's school and adolescent years. Here follows then an episode in 1978, of the last year of our working in Sussex. We had taken a group of children to a eurythmy performance at the neighbouring Michael Hall School; among them was a rather tempestuous boy of eleven, with marked leanings towards delinquency. We found that he was deeply impressed by what he *saw*, more even than by the content of the story that was being 'dramatized' in eurythmy. 'What wonderful movements!' he said with great awe. And, what is more, he was a different boy on the next day, even still on the one after that—more even tempered and harmonious.

Crafts

The various crafts that used to be the backbone of medieval life on the land have never quite died out in the West Country. What is more, here and there they are experiencing a revival. They are also finding their way back into school curricula. From the Steiner Waldorf School teaching plan handicrafts have, of course, never faded. But that they could even become a therapy is a fairly new perception. We found it to be so and chose it as the title of a day conference we were asked to run in 1991, in Aberystwyth in west Wales, 'Crafts as a Therapy'.

There had been an earlier day conference held at Newtown, east Wales

*Weaving at Peredur, East
Grinstead*

also asked for by the AWMC and which we had called 'Rudolf Steiner's contribution to the education of maladjusted children'. To this earlier conference we had brought with us our eurythmy teacher to give a demonstration, alongside our talks about the three seven-year periods in child development. We had been encouraged, on that occasion, by the reception of our presentations, especially when a member who summed up the day had ended by saying, 'Thank you for a day of reality!'

Returning now to the 1991 conference, we again thought that we needed to do more than just talk. So we brought with us four of our autistic youngsters complete with their equipment from the Basill Manor workshops—a lathe, a loom, a pottery wheel and a hookey-mat frame. They appreciated the warm reception their performances received and enjoyed the social evening, being part of the conference, when upper school pupils of the local Grammar School gave a concert which included the playing of Welsh harps. What was developed in our talks centred on the milestones of early child development. Can we understand autism against this background and help to balance it? I can do no better than to let Joan's lecture speak for itself (she had written it out for herself in preparation).

Clay pot making in Cornwall

Characteristics of the Autistic Child

Although I intend in this talk chiefly to concentrate on one boy and his development over a period of years, I would like to begin with a few general remarks about what is called the condition of 'autism'.

For any of us who have had much to do with this type of child, it is quite apparent that the incarnation-process has not taken place normally during the first few years of life.

The *normally developing child* follows a fairly *regular pattern*. In the first year of life it becomes gradually integrated into the world of space through movement, and this reaches a certain completion when at one year it raises itself upright and begins to walk. During the second year speech gradually develops and by about the third birthday the little child in calling itself 'I' shows a certain stage of the development of the power to think. We all know these stages well. The autistic child never completely passes any of these milestones.

1) Space.

The inability to orientate in space is shown by many features. In fact the movements of older autistic children are often bizarre continuations of movements of the baby below one. Rocking of the body, hand-flapping, rhythmical shaking of small objects and many other movements of the autistic child are all a kind of space exploration that cease in the baby when space has become an inner experience. A later stage is the inability to interpret two-dimensional as seen in pictures into three-dimensional reality.

2) Speech.

In the same way the autistic child never completely passes the 'speech' milestone. Again, there are all stages of this inability. Some do not speak at all, some remain at the stage of saying single words. Some go as far as imitation of simple phrases, and reach the 'David wants an apple' level, but do not go on to saying 'I'. Others cross this bridge, but do not come to the point of living sufficiently inwardly in speech to be able to *contract* phrases. For instance, they do not say 'yes' in answer to a question, but repeat the whole sentence. 'Would you like an apple?' 'I would like an apple.' A previous Peredur boy, who is now 24, drives his own car, manages his own affairs quite well, and is a valued employee at a watch-factory, but he still converses like this.

3) Thinking.

During the class teacher period, 7 to 14 years old, and later, how many of these children can ever develop a real activity of thinking, as opposed to a thinking that is really a mere reflection of what they have heard in their lessons? We all remember the *history* essay where two pages are spent in describing every detail of the king's *armour*, while the actual battle is dismissed in a sentence: No ability to distinguish the *essential* from the *non-essential*, and no real concept-forming ability. It is really a matter of *inwardizing*.

The autistic child cannot 'feel at home' in the world of space, in the world of speech, in the world of thinking. And from this feeling a stranger on earth stems a great deal of the underlying *fear* and *insecurity*.

I would like to turn now to John [not his real name, SWR], whose case is particularly interesting, inasmuch as he came to Peredur only at the age of 15, into the hostel workshop training scheme. He was brought to us from Smith's Hospital. He had spent some time in their autistic unit as a boy, and although he had spent a year or two in a maladjusted hostel and gone daily to school—IQ 130—he had had to go back to Smith's not long before we admitted him. Like all these children he moved and spoke in a wooden manner, held himself very stiffly, and looked much younger than his age. His chief social problem was violent attacks of temper, in which he was capable of inflicting severe damage on people and objects alike. When he was admitted, his mother said she hoped we would be more successful than the other school had been, as every term he tore his whole outfit of clothes to shreds in fury and she had to replace them.

We had a lot of this behaviour at first, doors being smashed, sheets torn up, his typewriter thrown at the wall, a suitcase sailing out of the window and bursting open on the coal lorry, etc.

Concurrently with this violent behaviour, John had many obsessions, in particular one for drawing perspective drawings ... He also typed out endless copies of rail and bus timetables.

Because John was still so young, we took him into the morning lessons of the eighth class for the first year and he began to learn to weave in the afternoons. After a slow beginning in weaving he suddenly took to it and began to enjoy it. When the pottery workshop began three years ago John, who had then stopped attending school, continued with weaving in the morning and did pottery three afternoons a week. He continued with the trainee's painting class, however, as well as other classes.

Turning to his pictures again, you will notice an interesting development. (A collection of drawings were shown.)

Joan with students practising speech and movement at Peredur

- Black and white perspective
- Coloured ink perspective
- Use of colour as flat surfaces
- Variations in colour-tone
- Perspective out of pure colour

It is obvious, from looking at these pictures, that John has ceased to experience space from outside, as a mathematical skeleton, and has an inward perception of it.

During these years he has improved generally. The attacks of temper have completely vanished. He is much less wooden, more capable of social relationships. He goes to evening classes in East Grinstead, and this winter has joined the East Grinstead Choral Society. Recently we were visited by a psychiatrist, now superintendent of a big mental hospital, who had known John as a little boy, and recognized him in the weaving room. He talked to him and remarked later that he had never seen an autistic boy recover so completely.

Now the question was: What has really helped John? He was already quite old when he came to Peredur, past puberty, and we don't usually reckon with such recovery at this late age.

Looking at this collection of his pictures last year, I realized it must have to do with the fact that he has now orientated himself properly into space and feels more at home on earth. But what has brought this about?

He is now a skilful potter and weaver—there are still limitations, it is true, but nevertheless he has achieved quite a skill in both crafts (examples were shown). Watching him working, I gradually realized the answer.

In both weaving and pottery you find complicated and complete relationships in all three directions of space. In weaving the feet move up and down on the pedals, the hands throw the shuttle from left to right, and from right to left. After each line the beam is pulled forward towards you and then pushed away again.

In making a pot, it is somewhat different. The leg pushes the kick-wheel with a to and fro movement, the two hands experience the continual right-left movement of the wheel and gradually draw the clay upwards. So for the same person to practise both crafts means that they have a harmonious and complementary space-experience with both the upper and the lower organism.

These crafts are more than an artistically creative activity. They are in themselves a therapy.

10. Work on the Land—Why and How?

Readers may recall the mention of the Steiner Waldorf Schools' Learning Plan from the earlier chapter 'For the Rhythm of Life ...' An introduction to farming plays an early role there. It features as a 'main lesson' subject for children of 8–9 years old. Farming, after all, is a basic element of human life on the earth; and the interdependence of different skills and activities also calls for a healthy social sense. Just because of the far-reaching mechanization in modern times and of the urban environments in which the majority of children grow up nowadays, a new impulse is now waking up widely to let the young have experience of the realities of life on the land and of the need to care for the land in an all-embracing sense.

The following excerpts are quoted from *Agricultural Literacy, giving concrete children food for thought*, by Dr Aric Sigman (2007). (By the way, this paper was laid into my hands quite recently by an ex-pupil of the Peredur School for whom the farming ingredient of his recovery process, some decades ago, had played an essential role!)

> Our research is just the latest study to illustrate that direct contact with the countryside and farms has enormous, measurable advantages for children's relationships with food. Improved agricultural literacy is an important weapon in the fight against obesity—a battle England needs to take on and win, as the fattest country in Europe (Dept. Health, 2006[1]).
>
> However, further encouraging findings indicate that contact with the countryside is linked with a variety of benefits quite unrelated to food. It now seems that there is a critical period of 'green' development in children when they derive benefits from rural contact. [Hence the inclusion, just mentioned, of farming in the Steiner Waldorf Learning Plan at an important stage of life. SWR.] Just some of the recent findings include:
>
> - Children with symptoms of Attention Deficit Hyperactivity Disorder (ADHD) are better able to concentrate after contact with nature (Taylor et al. 2001[2]).
> - Children with views of and contact with nature score higher on tests of concentration and self-discipline. The greener, the better the scores (Wells, 2000[3]; Taylor et al., 2002).

- Exposure to natural environments improves children's cognitive development by improving their awareness, reasoning and observational skills (Pyle, 2002[4]).
- Results for schools with outdoor education programmes show better performance on standardized measures of academic achievement in reading, writing, maths, science and social studies. Classroom behaviour showed improvements as well (Lieberman and Hoody, 1998[5]).
- A study of 120,000 children has found that gardening increases their self-esteem and reduces the degree of stress they experience (Waliczek et al., 2000[6]).
- Nature buffers the impact of life's stresses on children and helps them deal with adversity. The greater amount of nature exposure, the greater the benefits (Wells and Evans, 2003).

... Studies now talk about a 'countryside effect', which leads to 'superior attentional functioning' (Taylor et al., 2001[7]). But how can something as mundane as a tree or a meadow exert any biological effects on children?

The explanations seem to revolve around the way countryside greenery effortlessly engages a child's attention, allowing them to attend without *paying* attention. This is profoundly different to the arresting effect of, for example, television on a child's attention. One theory is referred to as 'Attentional Restoration Theory' whereby certain activities cause a temporary 'attention fatigue' which is corrected when a child's underlying attention system has an opportunity to rest. And natural green environments help in recovery from this attention fatigue, in part because they engage a child's mind effortlessly ...

The latest research shows that many children are now looking at more than one screen at a time, switching glances between the TV and the Internet along with mobile phone text messages. Self-discipline requires a child's attention. So when their attentional system becomes tired their self-discipline declines, but when their attention is revived by exposure to greenery, their self-discipline improves again.

Great oaks from little acorns grow, as the saying goes ...

- ... once-yearly pilgrimages to the countryside won't be enough to shift children's attitudes and behaviours to food. They need to get their hands dirty—literally. An allotment, home garden or even growing vegetables in plant pots can be a highly effective way of

Bringing the wheat harvest into the new granary, Peredur

raising children's agricultural literacy and shaping or changing their dietary tastes for the better.

- In addition to green fingers, children should also develop sharp cooking skills. One in five children never help prepare the family meal, which in itself is a great learning process for pupils unsure of how food gets from package to plate.

- Other basic food activities will also help children grasp where their food comes from. For example, involving children in choosing the contents of and packing their own lunch boxes raises their knowledge and cultivates a sense of connection and responsibility to their diets.

- The family meal is also an important point of contact. A study this year suggested that we now have the lowest proportion of children in all of Europe who eat with their parents at the table (Bradshaw et al., 2007[8]), with the majority of dinners eaten in front of the television. However, if families ate together more often, discussing their meals, food knowledge and concern would become a natural part of children's lives. Moreover, talking at the dinner table confers other benefits such as closer family units and better behaved children who learn about interaction through taking part at the table (Spungin, 2004[9]).

On 12 September 2007, HRH the Prince of Wales in launching the year of Food and Farming, drew attention to Dr Sigman's research.

Today, as most of you will know, the Year of Food and Farming has published some research into children's knowledge of the countryside, agriculture and food. It is pretty terrifying stuff and should make us pause for thought. Let me just remind you of some of the findings:

- Firstly, one in five children never visit the countryside—that means that more than one million children across the country have absolutely no contact with the land.
- Secondly, a fifth of children say they have never picked and then eaten fruit.
- Thirdly, children in England aged between 11 and 15 now spend 55 per cent of their waking lives watching television and computers. That is equivalent to about 53 hours a week in front of a screen—a rise of 40 per cent over the last ten years!
- Fourthly, we know that children without any experience of rural life are twice as likely to admit they don't know where their food comes from.

Ladies and gentlemen, it doesn't take rocket science to realize there is a problem. But I really do think we need to ask ourselves some searching questions, such as whether this growing disconnection from the land, from the natural world and from understanding the rhythms of nature, is part of the reason why too many young people are involved in anti-social behaviour, or far worse. According to Dr Sigman's research published today, children who have contact with Nature score higher on tests of concentration and self-discipline, and he reports that exposure to natural environments improves children's cognitive development. Above all, and this to me is the most interesting finding of all, schools with outdoor education programmes have better academic results and classroom behaviour. This, I can only say, is one of the reasons I have for so long been such a committed supporter of school farms. I do believe that they are crucial to the whole issue of how you can get people into the land again; just by getting your hands dirty, putting a seed in the ground or looking after animals ...

I remember Patrick Holden, the Director of the Soil Association, who grew up in London, telling me that it was as a result of just one visit to a farm when he was a small boy that he decided he wanted more than anything to be a dairy farmer. That is the sort of experience that should be given to every child. It can be life-changing . . .

At Peredur we have learnt that the care of the land is also the care of people. We all learn through doing and a farm is an ideal 'training ground'. Ever since the very beginning in 1952, land and its challenge had become one of Peredur's foremost preoccupations—and it had its beneficial effects. Before giving two individual examples of the Peredur estate, it is worth noting that our growth had been gradual and steady. First we were able to acquire, in stages, our neighbouring fields; that was how we became able to grow our first corn and mill it for baking bread. Then, in 1968, we were offered the opportunity to buy the adjoining farm of 160 acres. This was made possible through a generous loan from Jack Pye (now immortalized in the Jack and Mary Pye Trust, set up to help aspiring young farmers to get started in life). Another loan from one of our parents enabled us to build a bakery with the mill above it, as already mentioned in the 'Environment' chapter.

There now follow two quite different experiences of nature, first, one of an autistic youngster and then another of a delinquent youth—two

Sheering sheep, Peredur

extremes! The first one, hardly ever knowing where any of the things came from that he handled daily, just loved to watch the sheep coming in for shearing. Then to see them being shorn, their fleeces gradually 'peeling' off and the ewes emerging from their ordeal (for so he seemed to think) as naked as pigs, gave him great delight. In time he even learnt the rolling up of fleeces into handleable bundles, once again through being able to imitate others, rather like a young child is able to. Another revelation for him was the next stage of wool, to see the clean, fluffed up mound of wool being turned into just one unending single thread and being wound up on the bobbin. The spinning wheel worked magic! No, not really—it could be learnt; he mastered it! Another miracle happened: once the loom was threaded the two and fro of the bobbin being the 'wool-carrier' made what did not exist before—a piece of cloth! A long way from the naked, helpless little newborn lamb he had seen in the first place. Needless to say, both the spinning and the weaving came easily to the young man, once he had been shown. And with it grew both his self-confidence and the joy of understanding how one thing led to another.

The second story is rather different. A clever boy of 15 had been expelled from school for being violent, in speech and action. He often flatly refused to join in with others' activities. However, when asked to join us and help to straw up more lambing pens he did come along. He may have been just a little curious as to what was going on there but too proud to let on. Anyway, he did come and as we started to straw up more pens—lo and behold—one ewe was just giving birth! You should have seen the tough lad! He was so struck with the helplessness of that little newborn thing. I had never seen the lad in wonder, and that persisted as he watched in awe while the newly born—very gently—was put to suck. The innocent and helpless lamb had touched him deeply. But on the surface he remained a disturbing influence, so much so that we thought, for the sake of the others, we would not be able to keep him. 'One more term,' we said to ourselves. 'We will see whether things get better.' Well, they did. I had seen him (during one of my lessons!) pouring 'secretly' over a booklet on 'Bonsai Planting'. Would we be able to kindle his interest in the plant world altogether? Yes, Joan did, with her profound knowledge of plants. It was the sound of their Latin names that particularly fascinated the lad. We encouraged him to study plants and ornamental gardening. He caught on and seriously considered our suggestion to take a course on Ornamental Gardening at a London college. Could he not combine this with living at home again? His parents were delighted that he seemed to be finding his way into life. He did so well in his first year that the college suggested he should take a second year course of Advanced Ornamental Gardening, which he did. Before going still further, he went on a journey round the world and then took up further training. He ended up as the Estate Manager for one of the London Boroughs. He is happily settled now with a family of his own. After all, he had been a clever boy but had seen no purpose in life. When my wife died in 2003, he wrote me a touching letter of the gratitude he felt he owed to her.

After these two more personal sketches of farm experiences, we return once again to the wider world. Recent decades have shown how disastrous the exploitation of the soil can become. After all, there has to be *give* as well as *take*, and artificial 'fertilizers' are not the answer in the long run. This can be seen by those who have watched for a time the agricultural scene and the changing 'quality' of its products. We are blessed in this country by ameliorating circumstances, such as the climate on the one hand and by a traditional good sense on the other, at least on the part of a good many farmers and gardeners. The Soil Association has pioneered organic husbandry on a large scale and shown what can be done to maintain good soil conditions without having to apply 'artificials'. The biodynamic movement goes even further and has done so since 1924, by developing measures to not only keep the soil as it is in reasonable health, but to enliven it—in other words, to increase soil fertility and the quality of its products. It is some years ago that I spoke to the manager in charge of the Soil Association's research farm at Haughley in Suffolk. He put it rather bluntly: 'The Soil Association tell you what *not* to do. Your biodynamic teaching tells people *what* to do!' (By the way, I gather that the Haughley Experiment, due to lack of funds, could not complete their scheduled programme to prove the superiority of organically grown produce.)

The disastrous effect that artificial 'fertilizers' can have on the land in the long term is now seen in China, as their policy makers have come to realize. But to what effect? A document on this subject was handed to me by Alex Inman, who acts as an independent consultant to the Chinese Government. It was first mentioned to me by its author, during one of our study sessions of Rudolf Steiner's lectures on 'Agriculture'. Our conversation had come to note that agricultural methods can vary greatly in different Asiatic countries and certainly contrast sharply between India and China. Their dire straits and their openness to new approaches speak for themselves in the following excerpts of the recent Chinese Government statement, written by Alex Inman and his colleagues on the

Advisory Board, called 'Circular Agriculture and Recycling in China and the UK'. The reader must be forgiven for asking: What on earth has China got to do with the Peredur Trust in Cornwall? The answer may be discretely hidden in what follows.

> The notion of a 'circular economy' as envisioned for the People's Republic of China relates to a position where natural resources are, as far as possible, retained within the economy thereby minimizing the need both to dispose of and dump substances or objects once used, and also to reduce the exploitation of new resources. The outcome hoped for, in economic terms, is greater efficiency in resource usage and abolition of a perception that the environment at large is an 'externality' . . .
>
> England can be seen as leading an 'Agricultural Revolution' into modern history. It was generally regarded as starting in the seventeenth century when land management methods (including cultivation methods and water management), advances in soil fertilization and improved breeds of farm animals and strains of food plants occurred. Subsequently, a developing UK economy and considerations of national food security lead, from the late eighteenth century, to increased regional specialization in agriculture, expanding markets and long-term agricultural subsidy (Cook, 2010). Since 1940, the UK (and much of western Europe) were engaged in agricultural intensification that not only built upon two centuries of agricultural improvement, but paralleled the Green Revolution in Asia in terms of inputs to agriculture such as mechanization, agro-chemical inputs and improved strains of crops. The outcome has been the familiar problems of diffuse water pollution within water catchments, soil degradation and general negative impacts on the water environment, something that became apparent for some decades (National Rivers Authority, 1992) and with which European policy makers continue to struggle at the river basin level, through the Water Framework Directive (UKTAG, 2007) . . .
>
> In environmental terms the contamination of land, air and water in China must be minimized with the impact on human, animal and general ecosystem health reduced. Such endeavours are firmly based in the environmental '3Rs': 'reduce, re-use and recycle' (Tan, H. and Yin, C., 2006), notions familiar to western commentators, even if western practice remains far from ideal in this respect . . .

Here a fourth has now to be added: 're-enlivening the soil'. There are signs of policy changes.

... The Chinese Government is open about its environmental and recycling challenges and is looking elsewhere for models of sustainable development. Implementation of a 'circular economy' is now enshrined in legislation (Standing Committee of the 11th National People's Congress on 29 August 2008). Furthermore, not only is China criticized as an 'exporter of pollution' (and it suffers badly internally from poor environmental health), it struggles to feed its population entirely from internal production ...

China is the world's largest producer and consumer of synthetic nitrogen fertilizers, accounting for an estimated 31% of world consumption in 2005. Chemical fertilizer use is key to efforts to expand food production and ensure an adequate food supply, since 1970. From then to 2008, chemical fertilizer use increased from 2.4 to 60.1 Mt yr-1 (total nutrients), a 25-fold increase. By the 1990s concerns began to emerge over the overuse and environmental impacts of nitrogen fertilizers in China. A substantial literature has emerged on the ecological implications and behavioural drivers of nitrogen fertilizer use (Kahrl et al., 2010). One helpful economic argument is that the marginal productivity of nitrogen fertilizer use in China is declining. This is consistent with falling yield response per additional unit of fertilizer application (Colwell, 1994).

In the UK it has long been recognized that overuse of fertilizer is not only damaging to ecosystems, but that the practice is uneconomic to farm businesses ...

Several systems are proposed for sustainable agriculture, including low-input agriculture, minimum tillage and organic agriculture. Organic agriculture is a well-understood and well-practised system, so that as a 'hook upon which to hang one's hat' it represents a defined set of parameters. It is a production system supported by a philosophy that precludes the application of artificial chemicals to land; in its place organic manures and recycling within a single farm holding are preferred ...

Regulation of organic practice is through the International Federation of Organic Agriculture Movements (IFOAM), and FAO (Food and Agriculture Organization of the United Nations) presently promotes organic agriculture (Institute of Science in Society, 2011): 'The FAO Report points to further benefits such as better animal welfare, wildlife protection, avoidance of GMOs and pesticides, more jobs and less energy used...'

Organic agriculture is promoted in the UK, farmers deriving

In the granary, Peredur

financial incentive for conversion from conventional methods (Natural England, 2011) and there are both economic and environmental arguments that favour the practice. However, to see organic farming as an automatic panacea for reducing nutrient leaching to waters from agriculture requires scrutiny. Because the ploughing of pasture in organic rotations is commonplace in Europe (Armstrong-Brown et al., 2000) [This is no longer going unquestioned, SWR], there remains the risk of leaching from this. The over-application of organic manures remains of concern (Bernsten et al., 2006). But in general, indicators of soil sustainability from organic holdings are positive (Munro et al., 2002). Organic practices are promoted in China (China Organic Agriculture, 2011) . . .

Conclusions

The Chinese research and practitioner communities are focused on Circular Agriculture. Immediate adoption of 'big picture' conceptual policies such as 'catchment management' or 'zero carbon' will have to wait until a detailed analysis of workable options has been undertaken, even within the paradigm of 'Circular Agriculture'. What may be achievable in a Chinese context needs careful consideration; perhaps only the most obvious options are to be adopted in the short-term …

We would, nonetheless, encourage longer-term objectives, some of which relate to engaging with the energy sector (widespread biogas plants), moves towards a 'zero carbon economy', which relate to the development of catchment management templates.

However, mirroring international experience in a move away from 'top-down' regulation, we see a significant role for community engagement including the role of demonstration farms, in promoting the roles of circular agriculture and in promotion of BMPs (Best Management Practices) (including careful application of fertilizers). As a part of this strategy, the identification of land areas vulnerable to causing water pollution is especially important.

Widespread policies leading to land-use change may not be deemed desirable, due to the need to sustain agricultural production. Such might entail replacement of intensive arable crops with grass or other crops that generate less pollution. Yet one Chinese publication has suggested a localized imposition of buffer zones and reinstatement of wetland areas for nutrient and sediment trapping; these might remain on the agenda.

A good place to start is with a combination of economic and agronomic measures to constrain agrochemical use linked with the identification of 'vulnerable areas'. Within this framework, it is the view of the authors that in supporting practices such as land vulnerability assessment, adoption of sustainability/organic agriculture and economic as well as agronomic analysis of the real benefits of agrochemical inputs is something of immediate importance. Here process modelling helps to build scenarios of pollutant loading. The blanket adoption of BMPs would be something achieved through agricultural extension and advice and should be introduced at the earliest possible opportunity. Spatial and process modelling naturally has a role here, providing these options are not too time consuming, are workable and are not too demanding on input parameters. We furthermore propose one means to an end is that of demonstration farms in order to promote BMPs.[10]

It is at this point that the letter I have just received from Alex Inman will connect the conclusions reached by his research committee with our own work at Peredur. A living earth is becoming a worldwide concern.

3 May 2011

Dear Siegfried,

Re: Relevance of Tregillis Farm

I am writing to provide some brief thoughts on the relevance of Tregillis Farm as a demonstration of an alternative form of farming to the intensive conventional systems which typify most farming units worldwide at the current time. My work as a practitioner and academic researcher in the field of natural resource management has led me to the conclusion that mankind stands at the threshold of major challenges to food supply, depletion of ecosystem resilience and resulting socio-political instability. It is within the context of this viewpoint that I offer these words.

In short, conventional agricultural systems have become far too reliant on chemical fertilizers, pesticides and herbicides. At the heart of the green revolution, these inputs have been spectacularly successful at raising crop yields and reducing food poverty for millions of people. But these inputs are characteristic of an inherently unsustainable agricultural system reliant on the continued availability of these inputs which is not viable. Oil, a key component of chemical inputs, will run out soon and other inputs even sooner. Phosphate mines, for example, will become exhausted within a 100 years.

Feeding sheep, Peredur

Some believe Genetically Modified Organisms provide a future path to follow but ever more evidence suggests this technical fix is not the answer to our problems. In my view, the fundamental point is this—we must move away from agricultural systems which rely on external inputs to closed systems based on nutrient and energy cycling. Soil biology, so plentiful at Tregillis Farm, is a vital component to enable this to happen which has been completely forgotten by the advocates of conventional systems. Vibrant soil biology helps plants to access nutrients and minerals; it enables soils to hold moisture without requiring energy hungry irrigation systems and biologically rich soils are also capable of providing all important climate regulation services by locking up carbon from the atmosphere.

Finding a different way of farming will require new skills to be learnt and places where people can learn these skills through practical demonstration. This is where Tregillis Farm can play such an important role in the years ahead: by offering an educational facility to both agriculturalists and members of the public keen to learn more about the food they put in their mouths and how it gets there. At the time of writing, governments, scientists and farmers are increasingly looking for solutions to some of the underlying problems becoming manifest with conventional agricultural systems, and farms such as Tregillis will help provide the answers. Peredur Trust should be proud of such an asset.

With best wishes,

Alex

Alex Inman, SFEDI, MSc, BA (Hons)
Independent Consultant, Research Associate, University of London and University of Plymouth

10th May 2011

Dear Siegfried

RE: Working at Tregillis Farm

This letter is to add comment on how Tregillis Farm, thanks to over 30 years of organic management, is able to demonstrate that non-conventional systems *are* an option.

As we see before us, the current food system faces extraordinary challenges and these circumstances have been provoked by unsustainable farming methods. We have to take some very brave steps now.

Much more sustainable and durable forms of food production are now crucial because the way we have done things up to now are no longer viable as they once appeared to be. The biodynamic method of food production offers huge potential to meet the urgent needs of our time. It was this that Peredur Trust recognized right from the start.

Tregillis Farm is aiming to realize its potential by employing bio-dynamic methodologies. Biodynamics is a human service to the Earth and its creatures, not just a method for increasing production or for providing healthy food. It offers a different way of farming whereby natural resources are used ethically and sustainably. The resulting abundance of food stems from the right view and treatment of nature.

One farm on its own cannot provide all of the answers, but at least it can perform and demonstrate agriculture—not agri-industry—as part of a new food movement. Everyone has to work together and we all have to recognize the principle that Mahatma Gandhi observed so incisively when he said that 'we may utilize the gifts of Nature just as we choose, but in her books the debts are always equal to the credits'.

It is an honour, as a tenant farmer, to be steward to this land that will keep on giving for generations to come. Energy must be given to supporting the 'good' rather than the 'bad'; building the soil not depleting it. Relationships to the land must grow again. Whilst the farm produces food the offer for people to 're-connect' is there too.

With kind regards

Laura Wallwork

A brief addendum (SWR)

Rudolf Steiner makes a point in his lecture course on 'Agriculture' (which, by the way, the three of us are studying together at present) that a farm is the healthier the more it can be developed as a self-contained organism, with regard to all it needs, including the breeding of young stock.

It is encouraging that, having farmed since 1954, we have so far had no cases of any of the three past 'scourges': brucellosis, foot-and-mouth disease or BSE (bovine spongiform encephalopathy—also known as mad cow disease). Thank goodness a recent spell of TB was only brief.

May hopeful seeds of healthy farming grow into lasting fertility, wherever we are!

Notes

1. *The Health Profile of England*, Department of Health, October 2006.

2. Taylor, A.F., Kuo, F.E. and Sullivan, W.C. (2001), 'Coping with ADD: The surprising connection to green play settings', *Environment and Behaviour*, 33 (1), 54–77.

3. Wells, Nancy M. (2000). 'At Home with nature, effects of "greenness" on children's cognitive functioning', *Environment and Behaviour*, 32 (6), 775–795.

4. Pyle, Robert, 'Eden in a vacant lot: Special places, species and kids in community of life', in *Children and Nature: Psychological, Sociocultural and Evolutionary Investigations*, Kahn, P.H. and Kellert, S.R. (eds), MIT Press, Cambridge 2002.

5. Lieberman, G.A. and Hoody, L., 'Closing the achievement gap: using the environment as an integrating context for learning', CA State Education and Environment Roundtable, Sacramento 1998, *www.seer.org/pages/research*

6. Waliczek, T.M. et al. (2000), 'Using a web-based survey to research the benefits of children gardening', *Horticultural Technology*, 10, 71–6.

7. Taylor, A.F., Kuo, F.E. and Sullivan, W.C. (2001), 'Coping with ADD: The surprising connection to green play settings', *Environment and Behaviour*, 33 (1), 54–77.

8. Bradshaw, J. et al. (2007), 'An index of child well-being in the European Union, *Social Indicatiors Research*, Vol. 80, No. 1, January, pp. 133–77 (45).

9. Spungin, P. (2004), 'National Family Mealtime Survey', Raisingkids.co.uk *http://www.raisingkids.co.uk/btt_2005/press.asp*

10. Biodynamic Agriculture Association, Glos. GL5 1QG. www.biodynamic.org.uk

11. Arne Klingborg, the Swedish Connection and the Lanthorn Press

Arne Kingborg

'Life to the Land' could have served as the heading for the preceding chapter. In the event it was the title of a book we published and which had been written by our biodynamic friend Katherine Castelliz and for which she had asked me to write a Foreword. But then, how had we come to publish books, something we had never done before and for which we had had no training? It came about through Arne Klingborg, the Swedish artist, whom we had first met in 1958. That meeting was a seed from which a great many things have grown. This is what happened.

Joan and I had some days to spare on our summer holiday in Norway (we had a Norwegian boy in our Peredur Home School). So we said, 'Why not go into Sweden and visit the Cultural Centre at Järna?' So we did. While calling on Solbergahemmet we heard people practising music. 'We have a musical evening in Arne Klingborg's studio tonight. You can come to that,' said Gustav Ritter (who had pioneered this first anthroposophical home for children with special needs in Sweden). So, at the end of that evening, in fact just as we were going out of the room—having heard lovely music and enjoyed strawberries and cream—Arne came up to greet us. 'Can you tell us,' I asked boldly, 'how do you produce those transparent colour effects on the walls and wooden doors as we saw them earlier in the children's house called Mikaelgården? We need just that for our school building!' Arne readily produced an architectural journal and handed it to us. 'It's all in there,' he said cheerfully. But we were not convinced that this would be sufficient and so we asked, 'Could you not come to us and help us do it in our new school building in Sussex?' 'Oh,' said Arne, 'I have always wanted to go to England!'

This is how 40 years of inspiring help and fruitful togetherness began, with Arne coming over to stay with us twice a year, for many years (less often later on), first in Sussex and then, from 1975, in Cornwall. Good art and design lay not within our abilities but we appreciated them when we saw them. What follows is a brief account of some of the events that followed after this first encounter.

In autumn 1959, Arne came to England for the first time. He painted, together with our capable maintenance man, both the passage and the classrooms of the second wing of our new school building, all with great enthusiasm, giving all the inside walls a wonderful and almost transparent glow. In the evenings we began to have deep conversations about the Anthroposophical Society as a spiritual reality and as a transformation of the First Goetheanum building in Dornach (Switzerland). As to the origin of his special way of interior decorating, he told us how it came to be developed. 'There was a thought which Rudolf Steiner had formulated which moved and inspired us. It concerned the double function of a wall. On the one hand it protects and encloses but on the other it should open itself towards a new space beyond.' That is how the translucency of interior decorating (now referred to as 'Lazure') came to be developed. It was put into practice also in some of our other houses, both in Sussex and in Cornwall. 'This is almost like magic!' a visitor remarked.

In 1960, on 23 April, St George's Day and Shakespeare's birthday, we had the festive opening of our two-winged school building as already mentioned in the 'Environment' chapter. On the next morning the three of us set off to drive to Cornwall. Never will I forget the sunset of that day when we slowly descended into Tintagel, on the Bossiney side. It was almost like a sudden burst of trumpets when suddenly a vista sprang open of the most glorious evening sun becoming one with the red-golden sea. We were quite overwhelmed and just stood there transfixed. Arne often remembered that first experience in the coming years.

Later in that pregnant year Arne was in Dornach (Switzerland), the worldwide centre of anthroposophical work, preparing the 1961 Centenary Exhibition (Rudolf Steiner was born in 1861). When we visited Arne at his work we found him preparing a richly illustrated brochure of Rudolf Steiner's life and work, to travel with the Exhibition. 'Just the thing we need in England,' we said. 'Here you are,' said Arne, and handed us a set of proofs. 'If you can translate the text it can be printed here, together with the German version.' So we did and it has been a widely used introductory booklet for many years. We had no idea that this joint translation work was but a precursor of another, much larger task we would soon be called upon to tackle.

In 1962/3, as already mentioned earlier, Arne helped to prepare our Appeal brochure to raise money for building a school-leavers' hostel. At his suggestion we asked a number of well-known representatives of

English culture to lend their names as patrons of our Appeal to be printed in the brochure. Among them were Yehudi Menuhin, the Duke of Norfolk, Lawrence Olivier and Sir Patrick Moore. The Appeal itself was launched on 5 May 1964 by Professor Fulton, Vice-Chancellor of Brighton University, who ended his speech by saying, 'The principles of Rudolf Steiner are those of religion expressed in a practical way of life . . . The seeds sown by the Shaftesburys and the Nightingales and like-minded people have grown into a great system of social welfare of which we are entitled to be proud. But any system, however enlightened, must be challenged by fresh awareness of new and changing needs. In this the voluntary trusts like Peredur have an important place.' This was an altogether festive day, with the children performing the 'Peredur Play' which Joan had written. As for the Welsh name 'Perédur', readers may recall its first emergence in our searching conversations for a name well before we were able to start the work.

The fulfilment of the Appeal came two years later. It was the opening of this Swedish-designed hostel building by Princess Margaretha of Sweden, on 5 May 1966, with the Swedish flag flying from a newly erected mast outside the hostel. Enjoyable details—in spite of pouring rain—have already been given in the 'Environment' chapter.

Now to the publishing adventure already mentioned at the very outset of this chapter. In our work with school-age children we had felt a great need to find suitable reading books. Many of our children, late in learning to read, showed little interest in learning it from books with an uninspiring make-up and trivial content. Could we not remedy that? So Joan and Isabel Wyatt, an old friend and writer in her own right, set to work. They asked Arne Klingborg to do the layout and he inspired one of his gifted students to create suitable illustrations. 'Hay for my Ox', for ages 6 to 7, was the outcome and it really met the bill! It went through seven reprints all told, first in hardback and later in soft covers, beginning in 1968 and going on through the years. It triggered follow-on reading books for older children, first a collection of illustrated Norse tales for ages 9–10, with poems and riddles and a rousing song. It was called *The King and the Green Angelica* and also went through a second printing. A later reader (for 10–11-year-olds) was beautifully decorated, this time in the style of medieval manuscripts: *Tales the Harper Sang* was its name and it also carried a short version of the Peredur story of adventures and high hopes.

Quite a different need had also to be met and that was for more study material for those interested in biodynamic agriculture, both introductory and advanced. Among them were *Soil Fertility*, subtitled *Renewal and*

Preservation (having long been out of print) and *The Earth's Face*, by Ehrenfried Pfeiffer. *The Living Earth* by Walther Cloos became a classic for deepened study of the early living stages of our planet. It also became the rich study material for subsequent annual conferences of the Bio-Dynamic Experimental Circle, held for many a year at Peredur. *Life to the Land* by Katherine Castellitz—the very motto of biodynamic work—has already been mentioned. What was the most fruitful but also the most strenuous was the translation and publication of Maria Thun's annual planting calendar, which we managed to make available for 26 long years! We called it *Working with the Stars* because every year the different planetary movements and positions against the zodiac vary and so do their effects—favourably or not at all so!

Now we come to the biggest task of all which was *Education Towards Freedom*, Arne Klingborg's and Frans Carlgren's comprehensive and richly illustrated book on Steiner Waldorf education. No English publisher could be found at that time, 1976 (it would be different now!). But Arne's urgent concern was to see this so well illustrated book also in English. He persuaded Joan and me to take on both to translate and then to publish this major work through our Lanthorn Press. The translation itself took two years of our school holidays and the distribution was another job for which we were in no way prepared. But it all came to pass, although rather slowly. That book, in its latest edition, is now available from Floris Books as are others of our titles mentioned in this narrative. This *Education Towards Freedom* book continues to be a trail-blazer for Steiner Waldorf Education and has helped towards the founding of new Waldorf Schools, of which there are now over a thousand throughout the world.

In later years we extended our publishing work to include significant themes taken from history and literature. Two of these books were reprinted in 2005—*Shakespeare's Flowering of the Spirit*, by Margaret Bennell, and *From Round Table to Grail Castle*, by Isabel Wyatt. Arne Klingborg gave each its beautiful layout, and all the books carried Arne's simple Lanthorn Press logo. From the Shakespeare book I borrowed Stephen Spender's motto for this present publication and from the Round Table book Joan Rudel's introduction which follows herewith.

Towards the end of the 12th century Alanus ab Insulis, that renowned teacher in the School of Chartres, spoke of King Arthur in a way that was at the same time valid for his own era and a prophecy for centuries to come. He said, 'What place is there within the bounds of the empire of Christendom to which the winged praise of Arthur the Briton has not extended? Who is there, I ask, who does not speak of Arthur the Briton, since he is but little less known to the people of Asia than to the Britons, as we are informed by pilgrims who return from Eastern lands? The peoples of the East speak of him as do those of the West, though separated by the breadth of the whole world.'

This was written three hundred years before Sir Thomas Malory finished composing his *Morte d'Arthur*, still the most-used source-book of these stories in English, and eight hundred years before Edward Burne-Jones and William Morris, their imaginations fired by the Arthurian exploits, created the beautiful tapestries reproduced in this book.

Despite the continuing efforts of scholars and historians there is, however, no documentary proof of the existence of a historical King Arthur. Nor can anyone point with certainty to the physical where-abouts of Camelot or Avalon or Carbonek, or that mysterious lake from whose waters arose the sword Excalibar. Yet throughout the centuries and right on into our own times peasants and kings, saints and warriors, painters and sculptors, poets and musicians have found inspiration in these stories of the deeds of King Arthur and Knights and the interwoven theme of the Grail.

How can we account for the continuing and widespread interest in these legends? The answer to this question may have to be sought in a world other than in the physical world of time and space that man inhabits between birth and death. These stories have maintained their perennial appeal because they speak to the hidden depths of the human heart. They answer its longing for a world that does not partake of the transitory nature of our earthly environment, a world of eternally existing realities. The language of legend reveals the truths of this other world in great imaginative pictures. In the twelve studies of this book the author attempts to penetrate to the spiritual realities behind the happenings in the various versions of the Arthurian and Grail stories, as they are affirmed and illumined by Rudolf Steiner's spiritual-scientific researches.

In 1975 we again went to Cornwall together. We saw Basill Manor for the first time and were busy with energetic phone calls to the London agent, urging him not to let Basill slip from our grasp. At last, the contract was clinched and the Hayward Trust paid for its purchase. Now we could think about actual plans for Basill's future. Arne suggested that we used only the house for living and social activities, then all the outbuildings could be prepared for workshops. His later suggestion of the warm, strong plum colour for all doors and windows gave all the buildings a 'belonging together' appearance. Over the years, many groups of mature students from the Swedish Culture Centre came, for shorter or longer spells, to decorate various walls in our three Cornish centres—Basill Manor, West Tregillis and Trebullom—by using their well-developed 'lazure' colouring of many shades.

One more—rather adventurous—visit to the Cornish coast could be mentioned. It may have been in the early 1980s when Arne had been ill and Joan and I had urged him to come over and stay at our cottage, West Trespearne, to recover, together with his wife Gertrud. I remember one particular outing, when he was already feeling better and stronger. It was a wild and windy wet day when Arne said, '*Now* I would like to go to Tintagel!' So we did. Never before or since have I stood on the cliff just west of the headland, with the rain storm howling past us horizontally from the west to the east, and the waves below us throwing their foamy waters high up against us. We did not stay long—long enough to get thoroughly soaked! But it was a wonderful experience.

★   ★   ★

Basill Manor

When Joan had passed away, on 31 May 2003, I wrote a brief summary of
our Klingborg phase because—

> Arne Klingborg had hoped to contribute to these memories but, sadly,
> he is not well enough to do so.
>
> Joan was for ever grateful for Arne's artistic impulse, throughout 40
> years of fruitful cooperation. Hers were often the ideas and his the
> creations in colour and form, be it in the several new Peredur buildings,
> or in our landscape gardening or in book layouts. Joan went out of her
> way, in our many journeys, to acquaint Arne with examples of English
> culture, especially of architecture and garden designs. We in turn
> repeatedly visited the beautiful Rudolf Steiner Centre in Jarna
> (Sweden) of which Arne was a co-founder. We partook in a special
> conference by Waldorf teachers who came from this country to share
> in the developments of our Swedish friends. I was pleased to respond to
> Daniel Bittleston's request to write up a report of it which I include
> here.

What do we Mean by an Artistic Education?

William Morris (1834–96), social reformer, poet, artist and craftsman-
designer, was not only ever-active himself. He also inspired a circle of
friends around him, and even today his influence is still felt. The
Swedish artist Arne Klingborg spoke with appreciation of Morris's
impulse in his opening words at the one-week conference for English
Waldorf teachers held this August at the Rudolf Steiner Seminariet in
Jarna. The title of this article was the conference theme and a number
of answers were provided, in unexpected ways.

The conference programme was varied and relaxed. We did a lot of
walking and looking about, in the first place; we also practised
improvised singing and rhythmical games with Par Ahlbom, who is a
teacher at the Jarna Waldorf School; we did regular painting and
drawing, too. And the fact that all of us helped with the daily domestic
duties was just as much part of the conference. All these activities gave
rise to a mood that is not easy to convey. The pictures give at least some
idea of the new buildings that surrounded us, rising from the granite
hillocks as if continuing the motif of these rocky islands in a one-time
ocean, but now surrounded by pines and firs and birch coppices. There
is the tall Eurythmy House, its wooden walls and metal-panelled roof
painted a deep blue outside and a pale aubergine inside. Near it stands
the Library Building, angular and many-windowed and light green in

its exterior, then Allmandinen (with a music room etc.) with its domed roof surmounting the rounded knoll by which it stands. All three incorporate a flat, so that someone lives in each of them. The guests from abroad—and there were 36 of us—were accommodated in the three students' hostels, also newly built. They are a joy to behold and a pleasure to live in because every architectural detail is taken care of and translucent watercolours lighten up walls and furniture.

There is landscape architecture too. We took a walk round the sewage ponds on the first morning. As there are up to 250 people resident at the Seminar during most of the year and no main drainage is available a solution had to be found. The English sculptor and mathematician John Wilkes, whom Arne Klingborg met on one of his first visits to England, developed with him a scheme for revivifying water so that after a time it can again support successively higher forms of life. Theodor Schwenk's work (his book *Sensitive Chaos* is now in its third edition) was invaluable in elaborating series of sculpted flow-forms which enhance the oxygenating process by way of a number of water-stairs. My full article on this scheme, which has now been operating for four years under the supervision of Lars Fredlund, appeared in the *New Scientist* on 6 October 1977. It is remarkable to see how the variety and quality of vegetation and animal life increases as one follows along from the first pond right onto the fourth. The ecological value of such an enterprise becomes obvious when one compares it with the conventional sewage works in the nearby town of Jarna, where not only the buildings are bleak but vegetation all around has become practically sterile.

It is impossible within the compass of this article to do justice to the visit we paid to Stockholm. Readers will have to follow our footsteps—when they get the chance—to appreciate what we saw that afternoon: first of all the Kristofferskolan, Sweden's biggest, beautifully designed Waldorf School for which both town and central government gave substantial building grants; then the exemplary Kindergarten complex; and finally some splendid examples of Renaissance architecture in the Old Town.

Future visitors should also include, as we did, a visit to Mikaelgården, one of the numerous anthroposophical homes for handicapped children, again with most strikingly designed and—what was equally appreciated—lovingly looked-after buildings. From another curative educational home—Salta Arbetskola—have sprung a number of practical activities, agricultural and otherwise. We visited the mill and bakery—these mill and bake 800 tons of biodynamic wheat a year, along with attempts at new social forms of shared responsibility.

It completes the experience of the whole Jarna enterprise to see something of their five biodynamic farms, working 750 acres between them in a severe northern climate. Their latitude is that of the Orkney Islands. We saw Skillebyholm, which forms part of the seminar inasmuch as 22 students work and study there for a regular part of their two-year course.

Without the background of these various visits and experiences, the conference sessions themselves would not have been so full of life. Every day we divided into two groups for our artistic work, one group with wax crayons and the other with watercolours, often out of doors. Observing, yes, but copying—no. So what were we aiming at?

That was one of the questions that was fully dealt with in the course of the three evening lectures and followed through in the daily discussion sessions. Arne Klingborg developed in growing intensity a central theme of his life in art: Expressionism on the one hand—the little child is fully an Expressionist—and Impressionism on the other (that step must be taken as the child grows older). Healthy fantasy in the young child can lead to fantastic and even hallucinatory experience if it goes to an extreme, while good observation if it does not transcend the purely physical aspect can become dead naturalism. Blake and Turner are marvellous representatives of these two main directions in art and each was a genius in his way. We can see these tendencies in modern art as well, sometimes going to extremes. Herbert Read, in *Education Through Art* and other titles, draws attention to Schiller's *Letters on the Aesthetic Education of Man*. So does Rudolf Steiner, particularly in a course of lectures given in Berlin in 1905. He points out that these letters will become more and more important for people in the future, as a guide not only in art but in life generally, because of the questions becoming more and more urgent: 'How do I find a balance in my life? I do not want to live only out of preconceived ideas. I do not want to live merely out of primitive urges either. Neither way is creative on its own. How can I find a healthy middle way? How can I be free?'

If we awake to these questions we are also on the way to seeking a new art. And art in education will then need to be twofold. In the first place the teacher himself must become an artist. An impressionist painter transforms what he sees. The colours in his picture are no longer bound to the objects—they begin to speak, they sing (marvellous to see in the later Monet!). So must the teacher transform his subject and the facts he has gathered for what he gives out to the children to be born anew out of himself. The other aspect is what forms the *environment* of the growing child. That, too, must be transformed in every detail. 'If that is done with artistic feeling it gives support to the spiritual element in every human being who enters the school. Then schools will become what they need to be more and more (and what churches often used to be in the past): spiritual centres with a health-giving radiating power.'

A new way of living that will give rise to a new art penetrating the entire surroundings and in turn supporting and sustaining all people—that, after all, had been William Morris's dream. Not long before his death Morris wrote a kind of utopia and called it, somewhat resignedly *News from Nowhere*. 'News from Jarna', on the other hand, which is what this article has attempted to give, is most encouraging. This conference on 'What do we mean by an artistic education?' confirmed the hope that out of anthroposophical knowledge and experience real and far-reaching answers can be found and have, in fact, begun to be put into practice.

Their final achievement, years later, culminated with the festive opening of the new Culture House in which Arne insisted we should participate.

Students perform a play, Peredur

We did indeed, and here follow excerpts from one of the reports of it in Sweden's national press (*Svenska Dagbladet*, Tuesday, 4 August 1992, translated by Bjorn von Schoultz).

An Anthroposophist Receives a Gold in Pedagogy

When the Minister of Culture Birgit Friggebo arrived on Sunday at Ytter-Jårna near Södertalje to inaugurate the House of Culture newly built by the anthroposophists, she was discreetly equipped with an Illis Quorum medal.[1] In her very appreciative address in which she first of all referred to the complex of buildings and activities which the anthroposophists have created near Jårna as a pedagogical province she quoted the recently deceased writer Kerstin Anér as the one who had first opened Birgit Friggebo's and her colleagues' eyes to the anthroposophical ways of thinking. At this point she drew the gold medal out of her pocket and summoned a totally surprised Arne Klingborg onto the stage. Then, spontaneously embracing him, she pinned the medal to his lapel as a sign of the government's acknowledgement of his contribution to education ...

Arne Klingborg? The driving force within the Anthroposophical Society in Sweden and the one who is now responsible for the interior decoration of the House of Culture, an artist and teacher of wide renown ...

Anders Kumlander, chairman of the Anthroposophical Society in Sweden, promised that this House of Culture should not only be the focal point for the school of anthroposophical spiritual science but also provide a public forum that can contribute to a solution of the problems of the future ...

The most touching speech was made by Andrus Ristkok, a prominent member of the Estonian parliament. 'You have probably forgotten how difficult it can be suddenly to become free ...' he said. 'How, for example, is one to develop a new education without restrictions from Moscow ... Adding to the difficulties is all that now floods the Baltic region as Western culture and non-culture in the form of the soap operas, for instance ... How can we guard against it? How do we find our way?'

'It is refreshing to see alternatives such as those put forward by the anthroposophists and the realization of an experience such as we can see here at Jårna,' Andrus Ristkok said.

As regards my own experience of a decades-long acquaintance, I gave a very brief account of it when Arne had died and I spoke at his funeral on 5 November 2005.

> ... When the Peredur enterprise moved to Cornwall, it was also for Arne quite a challenge. Particularly striking were for him the experiences of being at Tintagel, on the rocky and windy north coast where King Arthur's castle had once stood. Many were our visits there, both in colour-filled sunshine and in violent rainstorms. The Arthurian efforts of taming the wild elements, both in the natural and in the human world, of transforming and ennobling the environment, were motives which we shared at quite a deep level. I remember he got really cross once, as I had never seen him before. It had been suggested to us to help organize a large scale family summer holiday party in Tintagel. It must have seemed almost blasphemous to him: 'No,' he said most emphatically, 'this is our lifeblood!'
>
> We are here to remember—yes. But are we not also here to make fresh resolves for the future? As a small gesture the Lanthorn Press (which Arne had suggested we should start) is to republish the book *From Round Table to Grail Castle* for which he had done the layout.
>
> To end with, I would like to turn to Arne himself and say quite simply: 'Dear Arne, may your far-reaching aims live on in our good will.
>
> Thank you for letting me say this.'

Note

1. *Illis quorum meruere labores* (To those whose endeavours deserve it)—a royal award established by the King in 1785, the highest award the government now grants for cultural, social and artistic achievements. (Translator.)

12. The Steiner Committee for Special Needs—Can We Think Together?

An immediate connection of this new chapter with the foregoing one lies in the fact that this Committee, founded in 1981, held one of its regular conferences in Sweden. A connection had already been made in the early days of this group of special schools with our Scandinavian friends when five of them had been invited to our annual conference held at St Christopher's School in Bristol in the late eighties. New welcoming flower borders had been planted by them in the grounds, two community rooms were beautifully painted in their newly developed colour technique and Arne Klingborg had given inspiring talks in the evenings. Rudolf Steiner's words sprang to life again: 'True art has always been an instrument for health. He who loves art and feels a genuine reverence for the human being is able to incorporate art as a healing force in all spheres of education.'

Anyone who has been in the presence of severely disturbed children and been subjected to their often uncontrollable noises will appreciate the answer I received from a senior member of staff when I asked her whether she had noticed any effect from the transparent art of colouring the rooms. 'The children are quieter now at mealtimes,' she said.

In 1989 then, our conference was held in Sweden. Although only a smaller group of our Committee were able to attend, the impressions of the architecture and overall environment that had been achieved over the years is unforgettable.

Other conferences, at St Christopher's School in Bristol and, later on, at the Peredur Trust in Cornwall, are also held in fond memory. One of the ones held at Peredur, in spring 1995, was on 'Issues of Moral Education'. The preamble of the programme was as follows:

> We have today on the one hand a dehumanized technology, which for several decades has been gradually encroaching into every sphere of life, hampering human creativity and initiative. On the other hand, breaking out of these constraints and exposed as well to undermining background influences, the unbridled human will gives rise to excesses of brutality and antisocial behaviour on an unprecedented worldwide scale.
>
> What elements in education can restore the balance and further the renewal of moral and social conscience in the individual?'

Another Peredur Conference followed a year later, in April 1996, 'The Twelve Senses—The Bridge Between the Self and the World'. Its opening challenge was:

> From the moment we draw our first breath we are exposed to the sense-impressions of the earthly environment. The subsequent development of soul and spirit as well as body, the unfolding of the individual's whole later course of life, depends on whether what is taken in from our surroundings by the senses is health-giving or otherwise.
>
> This holds good for all human beings, whatever gifts or dis-advantages they bring with them into earthly life. The developing childhood years are of course the most sensitive to these influences from without, but the quality of the environment continues to shape the individual throughout his whole lifespan.[1]

There were also other themes and other venues. One consultative group met repeatedly in London in order to prepare a statement for the Warnock Committee, which was duly submitted. It described the work done in anthroposophical homes and schools for those needing special care, be it for longer or shorter periods of time.

Another concern centred on training. What had been an 'in-house' training of young helpers and concentrated on the needs of St Christo-

Siegfried and Joan attending a SCSN meeting, Potterspury Lodge, Towcester

pher's School grew into a more formal course lasting for three years, with a full and varied programme as is described as follows:

Training Course in Curative Education
sponsored by the Committee for Steiner Special Education

Training in Curative Education
The study of the child with special needs is a necessity in the field of education. Rudolf Steiner's conception of man as a spiritual being coming to earth to meet and work out his destiny is fundamental to the understanding of the child in need of special care. Deviations from the normal development through hereditary conditions or other causes, and the resulting imperfections of the body, make it impossible for the human spirit to express itself adequately. Both the theory and the practical application of curative education are taught in the training course.

The Social Aspect
Right from the inauguration of anthroposophical curative education in 1924, this work has been regarded as a socially necessary service and, out of this impulse, some 250 centres of curative education and after-care working on the education principles of Rudolf Steiner have come into existence in this country as well as in Germany, Switzerland, Norway, Holland, Sweden, France, America, Canada, New Zealand, Australia and South Africa. Contact with the other centres is maintained through publications and conferences, thus providing an invaluable exchange of mutual experiences.

The Need for Workers
Workers in all branches of the care and teaching of children and young people with special needs are urgently required for schools, hostels and homes. The demand for properly trained people in this country and abroad is steadily increasing.

The Training Course
The Course is sponsored by the Committee for Steiner Special Education. It comprises three years, after which a Certificate in Curative Education will be awarded. This will be endorsed after a further year's probationary teaching has been satisfactorily completed. During the three years' course the students will become thoroughly acquainted with the principles and practice of Curative Education.

St Christopher's School in Bristol has provided accommodation and support for the Training Course for many years. In the first year students gain practical experience in the hostels alongside the training programme. In the second and third years there are ongoing opportunities for classroom observation and teaching practice. Block periods for full-time practice are also arranged either at St Christopher's or in other schools. The help thus given by students obviates the necessity to set a fee.

The course enables students to teach in Rudolf Steiner Special Schools in many countries. Students from this Course have also taken teaching posts in Rudolf Steiner (Waldorf) Schools for normally developing children in this country. Those wishing to teach in Special Schools in Britain may also require a state recognized qualification.

Admission

Admission to the course is not conditional upon previous academic attainment, although a good general educational standard is desirable. This course may also be useful for those with state teaching qualifications who wish to take up work in Rudolf Steiner Education. In some cases the length of the course can be adjusted.

Training Course Programme

Child Development

Normal and Disturbed Development; the Physical Background of Mental Handicaps; History of Education; Psychology; Anatomy; Physiology; Curative Education in the Home; Curative Education in the School.

The School Curriculum

The Three Rs; History; Geography; Mythology and Fairy Tales; Scientific Subjects; Astronomy, etc.

Artistic Activities

Eurythmy; Musical Games and Movement; Painting; Drawing; Modelling.

Music

Lyre; Recorder; Singing and Making Musical Instruments.

Craft Teaching for Children

Woodwork; Toymaking; Weaving; Canework; Puppets.

Home Care

First Aid; Home Nursing; Nutrition; Household Management.

After a time this training course could no longer be carried by St Christopher's on their own and the Committee stepped in by providing lecturers and course leaders from member institutions. Valuable work continued for some years but even that, after a time, could no longer be sustained. 'Training' is now once again becoming a subject for our meetings. This is now years later and under the wider umbrella of an 'Anthroposophical Curative Education and Social Therapy Association' (ACESTA for short). Our Committee, lately under the more appropriate name 'Steiner Committee for Special Needs', has now merged with that Association, in early 2011. Its venues frequently change as our Committee had done of late, both to make attendance more possible and varied and also in order to get to know each other's developments. The earlier quarterly is to be replaced by a new publication, *Point and Circle*, with the subtitle *Magazine for Curative Education and Social Therapy*.

Note
1. For more information about the twelve senses, refer to Steiner's lectures given in Berlin on 23, 25 and 26 October 1909 (GA 115). See *A Psychology of Body, Soul & Spirit*, Anthroposophic Press 1999.

13. Sustainability—How Far is it Possible?

In October 2001, Joan and I circulated a statement to interested people and groups that summarized our efforts thus far in achieving a measure of sustainability for the Peredur Trust and its people.

Provision For an Environmentally Safe Future
Water, Food and Warmth are Essential for Life

Water
When we took over the three properties Basill Manor, Trebullom and Tregillis Farm they only had somewhat inadequate spring water supplies. We upgraded these by employing local water engineers to install a new borehole supply in all three properties.

Food
The farm and the gardens together now can provide ample supplies, wheat for bread-making, meat, fruit and vegetables for human consumption as well as cereals for all the farmstock. All three estates are registered with the Dept. of Agriculture under one Holding Number and as such are certified as Organic with the Soil Association, both for our own satisfaction and for the health of the residents. It also enables us to sell surplus stock at better prices. Milk and butter are supplied by the small herd of Jersey cows kept at Basill Manor. We keep beehives on all three estates and grow herbs which play a useful part in the diet. The main greenhouses and food-processing area is at Trebullom. This is also where a new residential building incorporates on the ground floor a wood-fired bread-oven such as we have used for many years at East Grinstead.

Warmth
Central heating is basically supplied by Danish wood-fired central heating boilers. The cooking facilities mainly use Calor gas, but wood-fired cooking stoves for emergencies have been installed at Basill Manor and Trebullom. The newly acquired land at Basill Manor can provide an inexhaustible supply of wood for all purposes.

Power
At Basill Manor a refurbished mill-leat from the River Inney can supply a modicum of electricity by means of two hydroelectric turbines. At

A run-down old barn at Trebullom (top) is gradually transformed into a brand new bakery with a wood-fired oven

Trebullom and Tregillis Farm we are at present investigating the installation of two small wind turbines.

Although, of course, some of these works require capital input, the long-term effect is one of saving. Our variously skilled staff make it possible that all these ongoing developments can provide, together with the craft workshops and kitchens, interesting and enjoyable activities for the residents. Cornwall is providing us with an ideal environment, with its mild climate, fertile soil and the prevailing wind off the Atlantic which provides a relatively unpolluted atmosphere. What also helps is the friendly connections we have with local people, especially neighbouring farmers.

I reprint this report unabridged here to show what had been achieved but also the fact that it has not been easy in more recent years to maintain the level of sustainability achieved earlier. This is clearly due to a number of factors, which can be remedied and need not be discussed here.

However, two new projects have now been suggested that can now be mentioned here. One is to set up PVs (photo-voltaic cells) in close proximity to the bore-hole pumps on all three estates so as to ensure their continued functioning in case of mains supply failures.

The second proposal concerns the hydroelectric scheme at Basill Manor, which has gone through different stages throughout the years. The most recent proposal is now to regulate the water supply by laying pipes along the stretch of mill-leat serving the scheme. That would obviate the need to employ skilled maintenance staff to keep the open river water running freely down the leat. Such a project would need, of course, another substantial grant from an outside source. But that would be justified in view of the fact that other generous donations have already been received and are used for the making and installing of the self-controlled new turbine scheme itself, which is working well but is dependant, as explained, on a steady water supply. We are fortunate in having expert advice that we can call upon.

Further light is thrown on this theme of sustainability by the letters referring to Tregillis Farm printed at the end of the earlier chapter 'Work on the Land—Why and How?'

14. What are the New Needs?

Araminta Greaves writes her own impressions of the most recent project
the Trust has undertaken

The Peredur Trust and the Kernow Steiner Project

In 2003 a small group of like-minded parents and their young children
began to meet regularly for the children to play and for the parents to
discuss how to provide an appropriate education for their children. We
were all convinced that, unlike mainstream Early Years provision with its
emphasis on early intellectualism and a relatively rushed approach to
education, the Waldorf Steiner approach, with its acknowledgement of
the child as a multifaceted being with physical, emotional and spiritual
needs based on a deepened understanding of child development, would
be the best way of nurturing and educating our children. We also knew
that if we wanted anything other than mainstream provision here in
Cornwall we would have to do it for ourselves. Thus the Kernow Steiner
Project came into being. We continued to meet weekly with our children
and some of us also met regularly in the evenings to study Rudolf Steiner's
lectures, to plan how we were going to 'grow' our school and to develop
our craft skills.

After about a year of bringing the children together at various venues
including each others' houses and the beach, we began to search in earnest
for more permanent premises. After many fruitless forays down tiny lanes
to dilapidated village halls or near derelict old chapels, Kay Murphy, our
founding member, remembered that she had once been shown around a
hall at Trebullom, owned by the Peredur Trust. The hall had even been
used as a kindergarten some 20 years or more ago! We were very excited
about this development—but how best to proceed? None of us knew
anything about the Peredur Trust (except that it was an anthroposophical
organization), nor did we know anyone within the Trust. Kay and I
decided that we must arrange to meet Mr Rudel, the Chair of the
Trustees, to see if he could be persuaded to help our group to take the
next step into permanent premises, to set up a kindergarten for our
children.

I well remember going to Basill Manor with Kay one dark night, when
we sat by the fire in the hall and talked about all sorts of things with Mr

Rudel for over an hour, trying to pluck up the courage to ask about the hall at Trebullom! Having listened to all that we had to say about our fledgling 'Kernow Steiner Project', he finally asked the question: 'What can I do to help you?' Emboldened, we finally asked whether the hall might be available and if so, whether we could go and have a look at it to see if it would be suitable. Well, we need not have been so timid! We soon discovered that the 'Mr Rudel' that we had been so worried about having to persuade was actually 'Siegfried' who has been unstintingly supportive of all the Kernow Steiner Project's efforts ever since.

A few days after our meeting at Basill Manor, Siegfried took Kay and me to see the hall at Trebullom. It was breathtakingly beautiful with its warm wooden floor, translucent, pale pink lazure walls and stunning paintings that had been left there by Swedish students years before. We knew it would be a wonderful place for our children to take their first steps into their educational and social lives.

The local authority did not share our vision of the Trebullom hall as the perfect place for a kindergarten, mainly because the hall is the first floor of a converted barn so disabled access is a problem, and also because the toilet facilities are in an adjacent converted stable block. However, it has proved to be the perfect environment for 'Periwinkles Steiner Parent and Child Group', which has provided a wonderful experience for children from birth to five years old.

After a very successful and well-attended Summer Fair to launch the new group, Periwinkles opened its doors, full to capacity, in September 2005. Many families have come to Periwinkles and found something new to help in their wider family life: for some it is the idea of a candle at mealtime which helps them to keep their tiny children up at the table for long enough to eat their food; for others is it the revelation that outside play need not be curtailed by inclement weather if the children have proper waterproof clothing to wear; and for many it is the seasonally appropriate songs and rhymes shared when both parents and children come together in a circle for 'ringtime'. Outside time has also proved to be something of a revelation to some of the parents. The idea that the children can be involved in the necessary work outside from a very young age—as long as they are provided with appropriately sized tools—was new to many. I remember that the drive up to the yard at Trebullom often used to get potholes, so a favourite outside activity was for the children to fill the wheelbarrow with hardcore, and then a parent to wheel it to a pothole and tip it up so the children could scoop out the hardcore with their little spades and rakes to fill the hole. Once full it would have to be vigorously jumped on whilst singing: 'Here I am, little jumping Joan, when nobody's with me, I'm all alone'. Then the children would climb into the empty wheelbarrow to catch a ride back to the big pile of hardcore ready to deal with another pothole. Periwinkles children have been very fortunate to have been able to experience the progression of the seasons in such a beautiful environment, not only in the little meadow immediately behind the hall but also in walking round the orchards and fields variously in search of apples or snowdrops or other such treasures of nature.

People have often commented on the peaceful, nurturing atmosphere of Trebullom as a whole and this has become an important aspect of the Periwinkles experience for both the children and the parents. The gentle rhythm of the sessions helps the children to feel secure in a social environment and also allows tired parents to come together with others to share the highs and lows of parenting very young children.

Now, after six years and a vast amount of work by committed parents, the Kernow Steiner Project has recently launched its 'Sangreal Kindergarten', for 3½- to 7-year-old children, with a lovely May Day festival in the Mowhay at Peredur Trust's Basill Manor. The Kindergarten begins its life in what was a tearoom under the Weavery at Basill Manor with the Mowhay as its beautiful outside space. The Peredur Trust and the Kernow Steiner Project are working closely together to bring forth the next chapters in their stories—perhaps Cornwall's own Waldorf Steiner school! There is certainly a need for such a school and readers will be aware by now that responding to the needs of the time is what the Peredur Trust is all about.

15. Quo Vadis, Peredur?

by Paul Clark

'Wither goest Thou?' This was the question so often put or implied to those knights of legend as they set out on yet another quest.

How apposite, then, to address this to those who built their work and aspirations around the knight Peredur (or Parzival) of Arthurian and ancient Welsh Idylls.

Where, indeed? In the early days of Peredur Home School, there had been a growing awareness in educational, medical and social care circles that we were seeing—or maybe simply identifying—increasing numbers of what were then known as 'maladjusted' children.

There was precious little provision for such youngsters in the mainline facilities, and unless somewhere could be found where their behaviour and different abilities might be recognized and treated appropriately these children would face an empty and rejected existence.

In fact, many of them gravitated towards minor offences which saw them categorized as criminals. The Approved Schools of the 1950s and 1960s were seen as one solution, and the child for reason of physiological or mental 'difference' was often found edged into the system, via borstal, into a life of recurring incarceration in prison or psychiatric hospital.

However, as the foregoing chapters testify, there were some members of the teaching and care professions who took issue with the situation and dedicated their life's work and effort into bringing these children out of the confusion and emptiness of their lives. The philosophy and teachings of Rudolf Steiner had a wide-ranging and most impressive influence on many of these advances—not least of all, of course, with the founders and many subsequent workers of what was to become the Peredur Trust Charity.

The understanding of autism has progressed through the work of such places as Peredur and the many similar and associated organizations which exist today—on a worldwide scale. Awareness of autism has reached the stage where the UK Government has produced the 2009 Autism Act. We now frequently hear references to 'Asperger's Syndrome' and 'The Autistic Spectrum'. Until the late 1970s, at the highest levels of 'expertise', the word 'autism' seemed always to be linked only to childhood. It was as if the condition would disappear along with the coming of age at 18 or 21.

When this was accepted, albeit reluctantly, as a possible misconception, the first suggestions were that provision might be needed to be made for those individuals who had failed to 'recover' from that childhood ailment. Fortunately, until the professionals, the politicians and the powers that be moved forward in their way of thinking, the Peredur Trusts of this world continued to provide support, stimulation and care for their vulnerable residents—to an extent where many of the users of this service were eventually able to move on into society and the wider community.

This in itself was no easy task, especially when the various inspection, regulation and commissioning bodies were continually altering their requirements and standards.

And so, where next? For Peredur, as with those knights setting out on a new quest, we first need to be confident that our achievement is secure. Peredur Trustees and staff are happy that we can safeguard all that has been done to date. The Trust helped the parent and child facility 'Periwinkles' to become established in part of one of the properties—here is also where the main old listed farmhouse has been leased to a registered charity which provides respite care and counselling to people diagnosed with HIV and AIDS and their families.

Now we are about to embark on two further ventures. With the farm itself now leased to a young and enthusiastic couple who embrace the

Viewing goods for sale, all created by students, Basill Manor

ideals of organic and biodynamic farming, the Trust is left with a large unoccupied listed farmhouse building on the site. There are plans to renovate this and use it as a base and 'halfway house', providing a service for young adults with learning disabilities. Planning work for this is under way.

The second enterprise, which is due to commence in September 2011, is a Steiner kindergarten—initially on the ground floor of the Weavery at Basill Manor. The long-term aim is that, if this proves successful, we move on in partnership to establish a Steiner School in north Cornwall.

TIME ONCE MORE TO PICK UP OUR LANCE AND SET OFF WITH THE LANTHORN HELD ON HIGH . . .

A Brief List of Events So Far

Mid–December 1951	First six children admitted.
25.12.51	Three children celebrate Christmas with us, three others back home with their parents.
02.02.1952	Official opening of the Peredur Home School. The number of children soon exceeded the scheduled number of 20.
1958	Neighbouring fields bought which enabled us to grow the special 'Maris Wigeon' wheat for bread-baking. First young cattle and sheep.
February 1961	Support for the Rudolf Steiner Centenary Exhibition in London and, through the year, in 15 other locations: 'An Impulse for the Future'.
Autumn 1961	Fire at the main house.
1964	Appeal for building school leavers' hostel, opened by Prof. Fulton, Vice-Chancellor of Brighton University.
1967	Opening of hostel by Princess Margaretha of Sweden.
1968	Boyles Farm bought (160 acres) through Jack Pye's loan.
1970	Second Appeal for building a hall.
1975	Basill Manor bought for Peredur by the Haywood Trust.
April 1976	First group of five young adults, with a member of staff, start life at Basill Manor.
December 1976	A simple turbine scheme, using the mill-leat and installed by a local engineer, provides a modicum of electricity.
Autumn 1978	East Tregillis Farm bought ⎫ through the sale
Spring 1979	West Tregillis Farm bought ⎭ of part of the East Grinstead property.
October 1979	Trebullom Estate (11 acres) bought through sale of school buildings to the London School of Eurythmy.
1980	Changeover from Peredur Home School Ltd. and

	Peredur Farm and Craft Centre Ltd. to Peredur Trust.
1981	Rebuilding of Trebullom farm buildings.
1981	Foundation, together with others, of the nation-wide Committee for Steiner Special Education, later called 'Steiner Committee for Special Needs'.
December 1986/89	Shepherds' Play (staff and residents) in St Endellion Church and Lewannick Church.
July 1987	Both SWR and Joan Rudel admitted as Members of the Institute of Management, now Chartered Institute, after a one-year course.
1989–91	Refurbishment of Old Mill House into Weaving Workshop and Tearoom, with the help of a 50% grant from the Ministry of Education.
March 1991	Both Rudels granted Membership of the British Federation of Care Home Proprietors.
Mid-90s	Peredur hosting a number of Study Conferences.
2003	Decided to move from Care Home status to the newly created category of Supporting People.
2006	Despite meeting all new standards we were told that we no longer satisfied the new criteria of Supporting People.
2007	Being duly served with a notice of decommissioning we went to Appeal, and won.
2011	We continue as an accredited Supporting People facility. Three new applications from Cornwall Council for 'people whom we support'. The new Sangreal Steiner kindergarten starting at Basill Manor.

Who is Rudolf Steiner?

A Brief Account of His Life and Work

An opening theme

*Rudolf Steiner
(1861–1925)*

I quote from a lecture given by John Davy, principal of Emerson College, in May 1984 (he died in October of that same year).

Rudolf Steiner died in 1925. Towards the end of his life he gave a lecture referring to a modern phenomenon: for no obvious external reason, many people begin to feel rebellious about the times they are living in, become convinced that quite fundamental changes are needed. It is to people who are in this situation, perhaps quite privately, that Steiner can be really interesting.

In the United States, you have to be rather careful about using the word 'radical'. It is immediately identified with a pink, not to say red, kind of politics. Yet it really means to be concerned with the roots. The proper use of the word 'radical' is to indicate a conviction that the changes needed will mean uprooting some familiar things, will call for fundamental changes. In this sense, Steiner was a radical.

He was speaking, in the lecture referred to, to a fairly limited number of people—perhaps 200 to 300—in Stuttgart. He was describing this inner 'radicalism', and remarked that it would very soon be experienced by millions of people. He then described a kind of private drama which unfolds in many individuals when this radical frame of mind awakens.

The first act of the drama is, quite simply, that they begin to feel at odds with their surroundings. They have been brought up in a certain way of life, but now begin to say to themselves: 'I am not just a product of my family, my education, my times. Deep down, in my real self, I am looking for something quite different.' If we had more time, or were doing a whole workshop, I would invite you to look back in your own lives and ask: 'Have you ever been at odds with the world you're in? Are you at odds with it now? If so, how and why?'

This is the first act of an inner drama, which Steiner saw as belonging in quite a new way, to the 20th century to begin with.

Then he described the second act: 'The first act launches many people into a search. Now they don't want to believe that they are the only people who are thinking 'radically', they start looking for others who think as they do. If and when they succeed, it is an enormously supportive experience. Out of this, all kinds of societies or groups grow up. There are now in this country, throughout Europe, and in many other parts of the world, perhaps tens of thousands of groups of people who are looking for something different. The search leads to a forming of groups or communities whose existence could not be predicted from studying the orthodox environment. They emerge from something which stirs quite deeply within human beings.

The third act of this drama, as Steiner described it, opens when individuals and groups begin to feel that it is not enough to have a club or a society. Something must be done in the world at large. It is then, when we come to the threshold of action in the world, that life can become very dramatic indeed...'

I let John Davy's opening remarks also be mine. What follows, in my case, is a mere framework of Rudolf Steiner's biography. He wrote himself the first part of it in *The Course of My Life* but was unable to finish it. I also quote contributions by others, as well as some noteworthy newspaper reports of the times.

Features of the early years

Rudolf Steiner was born on 27 February 1861 in Kraljevic, on the borders of Austria and Hungary (now part of Croatia), where his father was stationmaster for the Austrian railway. While the boy took a keen interest in the developing technology of the time (the telegraph was just coming into use) it was a simple and rural environment in which he grew up. An early experience at the age of seven first made him aware of the reality of a spiritual world behind the physical world. But he could not share this growing awareness with other people for many years to come. At 16, he began his own philosophical readings and then studied science at the Technical College in Vienna. During this period he also undertook the teaching of a ten-year-old boy who suffered from a severe hydrocephalic condition and who, after two years' tuition, was able to join the grammar school, then study medicine and become a medical doctor. 'At that time I had my actual training in physiology and psychology,' Rudolf Steiner wrote in his autobiography. At 22, he was given the task of editing Goethe's scientific writings.

Finding a balance between impulse and duty

While his years in Vienna (1879–89) were also a time of lively social intercourse with contrasting circles of people, the period that followed in Weimar (where Goethe had lived) was often one of great loneliness. He had been asked to go there and help prepare a Complete Edition of Goethe's works. During these years he struggled to find a way of reconciling his knowledge of the supersensible world with the world which he shared with his contemporaries. It did not seem impossible to Rudolf Steiner to show a path that led to supersensible experience through the realm of the thought-life. He had already written his doctorate thesis 'The Fundamental Problem of a Theory of Knowledge' (1886). Thus he had prepared the ground for what still today is his fundamental book, *The Philosophy of Spiritual Activity* (1893) which in a recent translation is called *Intuitive Thinking as a Spiritual Path—A Philosophy of Freedom*.

At about 35, shortly before he left Weimar to move to Berlin, a decisive change occurred in his life. Attentiveness to the physical world and all its details which had not always been easy for him awakened in him to a full and most satisfying degree. 'In serving the physical world, one goes completely outside oneself, and just by reason of this one returns with an intensified capacity for spiritual observation into the spiritual world.' His life of meditation led him to develop 'the consciousness of an inner man who, in complete detachment from the physical organism, can live, perceive and move within the spiritual'.

Years of crisis and decision

The years in Berlin were marked by quite new challenges. One of them was the request to lecture in the Workers Educational Institute. This developed beyond the original subjects of history and evolution to scientific and social topics and was much appreciated. In fact he was asked, on the occasion of the 400th Gutenberg anniversary, to give the jubilee lecture to 7000 printing workers in a large Berlin circus building.

'Conceptions of the World and of Life in the Nineteenth Century' was the title of a book Rudolf Steiner wrote at that time. He later extended it into a history of philosophy and republished it as *Riddles of Philosophy* (1914). But it has to be seen that the early years in Berlin (1897–1900) were marked by two main factors. On the one hand there was poverty and the continuing struggle to develop the wide-ranging 'Magazine for Literature' which Steiner had taken over as editor. On the other hand there was an inner 'probation of the soul', so movingly described in his autobiography. What he himself was striving for and what came to meet him from outside faced each other in the years before the turn of the century as two opposing forces whose clashes were a threat to his outer and even his inner existence. In his autobiography Steiner says: 'In this time of testing I succeeded in progressing further only when in spiritual vision I brought before my mind the evolution of Christianity.' And 'the unfolding of my soul rested upon the fact that I had stood in spirit before the Mystery of Golgotha in most inward, most earnest solemnity of knowledge'. His book *Christianity as Mystical Fact* (1901) marked the point at which he had won through in this phase of 'most intense spiritual tests'.

The various lectures leading up to it had been held in a circle of members of the Theosophical Society. 'It must be borne in mind that outside of those circles, there was in the world at large no interest whatever for genuine spiritual research,' Rudolf Steiner explained in a later lecture (1923). While his connection with the Theosophical Society continued for several years (he was even, for some of these years, General Secretary of its German Section) it was not an association which could last. The independence of his own research had to be maintained as distinct from the growing tendency by leaders of the Theosophical Society to adhere to Eastern traditions. 'Anthroposophy' was the name which Steiner increasingly began to use. He meant by this designation the inwardly strengthened and practised consciousness by which a human being can experience himself as citizen of a spiritual world. He once elaborated this concept by calling it 'my consciousness of being human'.

Fundamental anthroposophical books 1902–09

It was in 1902, in a lecture to members of the Giordano Bruno Union, that Steiner for the first time had declared publicly his life's aim, namely 'to found new methods of spiritual research on a scientific basis'. The years that followed saw him lay the foundations of such work, both through the lectures he gave and the books he now wrote. The first to be published, in 1904, was an 'Introduction to the Supersensible Knowledge of the World and the Destination of the Human Being', this being its descriptive subtitle (the main title *Theosophy* is still in use today). In this book Steiner forges a philosophical path to the idea of reincarnation (Ch. 2) which through his spiritual perception was already a reality for him.

The second publication was a series of articles on inner development, now known under the title *How to Know Higher Worlds—A Modern Path of Initiation*. Its first sentence sounds the keynote: 'There slumber in every human being faculties by means of which he can acquire for himself a knowledge of higher worlds.'

These two books were followed by a third, *An Outline of Occult Science* (1909), now also known as *An Outline of Esoteric Science*. The title could have been misleading. It is, of course, not a question of the knowledge itself being occult, i.e. hidden. After all, it was being published as a book. But it describes knowledge of that which is normally hidden, i.e. from ordinary sense-perception. This book gives, from the widened viewpoint of spiritual research, a systematic description of the spiritual nature of the human being and of his evolutionary stages within those of the world as a whole. In this book, too, we find a chapter on inner training.

What is contained in these (and other) fundamental books is not so much a personal document, but an objective presentation in thought-form of a world not easily accessible to the untrained mind. These books are written in such a way that the thorough study of them is a training of thought in itself and thus a preparation for the reader's own esoteric development. It must always be emphasized that the path of inner development pointed out by Rudolf Steiner, unlike some other more mystically inclined movements of today, rests on the basis of clear thinking. In his Preface to the 1925 edition of *Esoteric Science—An Outline* Rudolf Steiner wrote the following:

'The books *Theosophy* and *Esoteric Science* have been widely read, though they count not a little on the reader's good will. For it must be admitted, they are not written in an easy style. I purposely refrained from writing a 'popular' account, so-called. I wrote in such a way as to make it necessary to exert one's thinking while entering into the content of these books. In so doing, I gave them a specific character. The very reading of them is an initial step in spiritual training, inasmuch as the necessary effort of quiet thought and contemplation strengthens the powers of the soul, making them capable of drawing nearer to the spiritual world.'

The role of art

In the Theosophical Society there was little interest in art. But just as ideas speak to the *mind,* so do truly artistic creations and activities engage the *whole* human being.

It was recitation and dramatic presentations which, through Marie von

Sivers, first became part of anthroposophical meetings and conferences. Then other art forms such as painting, sculpture and architecture were used first in smaller and then in larger building designs. These became forerunners of the monumental edifice of the Goetheanum, near Basel in Switzerland, which Steiner designed. It was constructed entirely through donations and with the help of a large international group of artists throughout the years of the First World War. Its principle form was that of two large intersecting domes, the smaller forming the stage and the larger the auditorium. All arts found expression here. There was also now a new art of movement (eurythmy) which was being developed as a visible manifestation of music or the spoken word.

Eurythmy also played an essential part in the performance of Rudolf

Steiner, working on his sculpted model 'The Representative of Humanity'

Steiner's four Mystery Plays which express in dramatic form the reality of repeated earth-lives.

It was a tragedy of enormous consequences that this building was destroyed by fire, on New Year's Eve 1922/23. A second Goetheanum building, quite newly conceived and based on Steiner's sculptured model, serves today as the centre of the worldwide anthroposophical movement. The development of 'organic architecture' and its allied arts, initiated by these two buildings, is continuously carried forward in many countries (see also Klingborg et al., *The Goetheanum, Rudolf Steiner's Architectural Impulse*).

Practical activities

It is the *practical* activities arising from his work through which Rudolf Steiner's name is now best known, especially in the English-speaking world. All of these spring from the heart of anthroposophy and their beginnings are rooted in Rudolf Steiner's own biography. With this chapter we reach into our own time and into the years to come.

The Waldorf School movement

It is important to note that, as an example of a free spiritual life, the first Waldorf School, in 1919, came about as the final fruit of a tremendous effort on the part of Rudolf Steiner and some of his collaborators, immediately after the First World War, to give the ordering of the social life in Middle Europe a deliberate new impulse. This was the idea and the practical proposition of a threefold social order with the *spiritual life* (e.g. education) on the one hand and the *economic* sphere with all its associations on the other hand, both becoming independent of the state and the latter functioning to ensure the democratic *rights of people*. These proposals were put before some European statesmen but failed to be accepted in their entirety. They need to be thoroughly studied so that they can perhaps come to fruition at a future stage (see Rudolf Steiner, *Towards Social Renewal*).

As for the Waldorf School movement itself, this has now grown worldwide and comprises more than a thousand schools throughout five continents, as mentioned earlier, with an even greater number of pre-school kindergarten foundations. The reader will find titles of various books and lecture-courses on education by Rudolf Steiner and other writers in the section 'Further Reading' (p. 167). Foremost is the richly illustrated volume by Frans Carlgren *Education Towards Freedom* (for its colourful history see Chapter 11). But see also—as an 'outsider'—the official assessment of *Steiner Schools in England* (Research Report RR645 authorized in 2005 by the Department of Education and Skills). Both of these, along with others, are available through the Steiner Waldorf Schools Fellowship at Forest Row, Sussex.

The original school had begun its life in 1919 through the initiative of Emil Molt, the director of the Waldorf Astoria cigarette factory, as a school for the children of his workers. From its very beginning Rudolf Steiner was its mentor and ongoing director. It was through him that the first group of teachers were enlisted and instructed throughout three concurrent lecture-courses to take on the development and administration of this first 'Waldorf School'.

It was my own good fortune to attend the final three years of my education at that school. The reader may recall both the serious and amusing anecdotes in the second part of my life-story. I was back in these old haunts not so long ago, when, in the autumn of 2009, I took part in the 90th anniversary meeting of the founding of that first of so many Steiner Waldorf Schools. After all, I had been taught in my time by a number of the original teachers and in later years Peredur had been visited by several of them, as mentioned in an earlier chapter. Now I was back, with people of all ages, and one particular discussion session was striking when four present pupils of the upper school shared the platform with the chairman and were encouraged to fire questions at us. I queried their interest in asking us 'oldies' about our lives: 'Would it not be more apposite to question past pupils nearer your own age?' 'No, we would like to hear more from those who have lived a whole life with the fruits—or otherwise?—of their Waldorf School years.' A highlight of the whole occasion was the 'Monthly Assembly', a feature of Waldorf Steiner School life, especially repeated for the hall full of visiting former pupils. Their orchestra excelled in accompanying their brilliant soloist in playing Mendelssohn's Violin Concerto. Different classes, from six-year-olds to young people of 18 years performed. There were rhythmical games and eurythmy exercises, choral singing, gymnastics—all delivered with astonishing ease and enthusiasm. On the next morning visitors could also apply to sit in on various classroom activities. My wife and I were allotted a science class 11 (16-year-olds) of mixed gender. The lesson started by all speaking a morning verse together with their teacher (as we had always done in my time!). The first part of the lesson struck me as being remarkably easygoing. But it was clear that the subject matter had been well understood. When it came to opening their notebooks silence fell, until individuals were called up to read out what they had written down at home. Conversation ensued. Then a new aspect was presented by the teacher which was received with marked attention.

The afternoon was given over to wandering around and visiting the display of paintings and sculptured work by older pupils. There was a final discussion session of present-day tasks and challenges, such as the increasing drive for lowering the age of formal schooling. So much for my experience of '90 Years Waldorf School' festivity.

An anecdote from the earlier time when Peredur was still a school may conclude this section. We always took the date of Rudolf Steiner's birthday, 27 February, as an opportunity to make the children aware of who he was and what he did. For many years we were able to ask someone to speak to them who had actually met Rudolf Steiner and spoken to him. One of them was Helen Fox, who was a founder, with others, of the Michael Hall School, in whose neighbourhood we had settled in 1951, with our future collaboration in mind. She had in fact met with Rudolf Steiner on several occasions. In what follows she describes such an occasion (published in *A Man Before Others*).

I was fortunate enough to have a private talk with him, and on three or four subsequent occasions. In the space of a few minutes, one's questions and problems were answered—or rather, one was shown a new goal in life and how to set about finding the way to it.

During the next few months our little group of would-be teachers met more often, and gradually and hesitantly the thought was born in us: 'Could we not perhaps start a day school in London?'

Then, on New Year's Eve, 1922/23, came the terrible tragedy of the burning of the first Goetheanum. (The fire started in the room where we had had our lecture-course a year before.) All the artistic and dedicated work of Rudolf Steiner and his many helpers was destroyed in a single night. I once heard a German teacher, who now holds a leading position in a school in north Germany, tell of how as a young man he happened to be in Dornach at the time and found himself standing next to Rudolf Steiner, watching the destruction. And then Dr Steiner turned to him and said: '*Nicht wahr, wir wollen weiter arbeiten.*' (We will go on working, will we not.) So the resolve for the future was already taken ...

A digression: A few years ago I was asked to speak at a school for 'maladjusted' children, on Rudolf Steiner's birthday. I told them this story, and when the talk was over I overheard one little boy retelling it with great gusto to his friends: 'And there stood Dr Steiner, watching how the whole thing was going up in flames, and—(with a jerk of the elbow)—he says to his mate, he says: " 'Ere, come on, we've got to get on with it!" ' Apart from the humour, it was touching to see how a little boy's heart warmed to Rudolf Steiner's courage.

Steiner education for special needs

Its beginnings were quite an independent departure, in 1924. It was in answer to the urgent questions of three young students working with severely handicapped children that Rudolf Steiner gave his first indications regarding both the understanding and the education of such children whose development is hampered by their physical and physiological constitution. A course of 12 lectures followed—*Education for Special Needs*, also known as the 'Curative Education Course'. It laid the foundations of what came to be called Curative Education, now a worldwide movement. It was led in its early stages by Dr Wegman, Rudolf Steiner's medical collaborator. There is a lively account of its simple beginnings in the collection of articles already mentioned, *A Man Before Others*, which is entitled 'The Beginning of Curative Education', by Albrecht Strohschein. This name will already be familiar to the reader from the second part of my life-story. There are now 646 establishments in 44 countries which are working on an anthroposophical basis.

Biodynamic farming and gardening

Concern about the decreasing quality of foodstuffs had led some farmers to ask Rudolf Steiner certain searching questions. Others were troubled by the dwindling viability of seeds and still others by problems of animal health. Steiner's answers to these various questions culminated in a course of eight lectures—*Agriculture*—given at Koberwitz in Silesia (now part of Poland), at the urgent request of Count Keyserlingk in June 1924. This course bore the seeds of what has now grown into the worldwide biodynamic movement of farming and gardening. To enliven the soil itself was one of its main themes, taking notice of the differentiated cosmic influences of stars and planets when working on the land.

While Rudolf Steiner gave immediate practical advice which would help to restore and maintain harmony in the landscape and quality of foodcrops he also suggested that ongoing research should underpin and substantiate what he had outlined. This has been done, among many others, by Ehrenfried Pfeiffer in the USA who also wrote fundamental books on soil fertility and ecology. Present-day research on the influence of cosmic constellations on plant growth is carried on in various places, e.g. by Maria Thun in Germany, resulting in her annual Sowing and Planting Calender used in Europe as well as overseas. There are now 4525 farms and market gardens in 47 countries comprising of a total of 142,482 hectares and 458 processors working along biodynamic lines.

There is a biographical connection between the two last-mentioned enterprises, which Rudolf Steiner helped get on their feet: the future biodynamic work for Farmers and Gardeners and the foundation on which the work with those with special needs can be built. It is significant that he travelled immediately after the Agriculture Course was concluded, on 17 June 1924, from the eastern part of Germany (now part of Poland) right across to western Germany (Jena), even though his own health was already a matter of concern for his friends. He felt deeply connected with both initiatives: care of the land—from his own childhood experiences— and stepping in where special help was needed—from the tutoring in his student days (see Features of the Early Years). Guenther Wachsmuth in his early *Life and Work of Rudolf Steiner* (1955) relates how he accompanied Rudolf Steiner on many of his journeys:

> Before returning to Dornach Rudolf Steiner went once more to Jena and Stuttgart. He had again requested me to accompany him on this trip, and I still remember vividly how, during the journey between Breslau and Jena, after a period of silent reflection . . . he said suddenly with a strong and joyful emphasis: 'Now we have accomplished also this important work.' Seldom have I seen him so joyfully moved after the completion of a task as in this moment after the agricultural conference.

Medical work

One more special 'theme' must be mentioned and that is the new medical work that developed in collaboration with open-minded medical doctors. Thus the last five years of Rudolf Steiner's life became increasingly marked by his concern for questions of health and healing, both in public lectures and in intensive work with medical doctors who had sought his advice. He was able to characterize different polarities of forces in the human organism and show ways of counterbalancing one-sidednesses. Disharmonies between the soul-and-spirit being of a person and their physical and life processes, both in general terms and through individual diagnoses, were shown to be frequent causes of illness. All this had to be thoroughly understood and taken up into 'a will to heal' and carried into daily practice by medical practitioners.

One of Steiner's close collaborators was the Dutch doctor Ita Wegman who founded a hospital in Arlesheim (near Basel, Switzerland), now named after her. The book *Extending Practical Medicine—Fundamental Principles based on the Science of the Spirit* was written jointly with her. Through an intimate knowledge of plant and mineral substances and their relation to the human organism new medicines and therapies were worked out, also for the treatment of cancer. Anthroposophical medicine, which augments the generally recognized medical work, has been developed further over the years and is practised in many different countries.

There are other practical activities arising from Steiner's work but they cannot all be described here.

Rudolf Steiner in England

The visits to England fall into distinct groups.

The early lectures were given in the first place to the Theosophical Congress in London (1903) and others to members' groups in 1913.

Steiner's later activities in England were concentrated into the last three years of his life when he came to this country no less than five times and often for several weeks at a stretch. Of these the public events in 1922 to which Steiner was asked to contribute were the most outstanding. It was through the untiring efforts of the English sculptress Edith Maryon that the pioneering educational work at the Stuttgart Waldorf School had come to the notice of Professor Millicent Mackenzie (University of Cardiff) who had then arranged a visit of a party of English teachers to the anthroposophical centre at Dornach, near Basel, Switzerland. That is when Steiner gave his so-called Christmas Course for Teachers (1921). The immediate result was an invitation by the group called 'New Ideals in Education' for him to participate in the Shakespeare Conference at Stratford-on-Avon on the theme 'Drama and Education', in April 1922. George Adams, in the anthology *A Man Before Others—Rudolf Steiner Remembered*, reported that 'Steiner was invited both as an educationalist and as a distinguished authority on Goethe. His two lectures aroused such interest that he was asked to give a third. He was here speaking side by side with foremost representatives of English life and letters, John Masefield and John Drinkwater among them. I remember the latter at a social gathering asking me many questions about Rudolf Steiner.' *The Times* (29 April 1922) referred to the fact that 'the famous person in this year's conference was Dr Rudolf Steiner who is distinguished at present, not only in the field of education but also in other fields . . .'

An even larger public conference, this time on 'Spiritual Values in Education and in Social Life', was arranged at Oxford later that year (August 1922), again with Professor Mackenzie as one of the organizers. It was held at Manchester College and its principal Dr L.P. Jacks opened the two weeks' conference at which Steiner gave the morning course of lectures. The *Oxford Chronicle* (18 August 1922) remarked that '200 students are taking part in this. Presiding at the Conference is the Minister for Labour, Dr. H.A.L. Fisher and prominent representatives of the most varied special fields are included in its council . . . The Programme thus comprises an extensive area of pedagogical ideals and endeavours . . . The most prominent personality at this congress is probably Dr Rudolf Steiner . . . (who) speaks every forenoon on "The Spiritual Foundation of Education".'

It is noteworthy that this conference also included lectures by teachers from the Stuttgart Waldorf School as well as varied artistic demonstrations. On the final day (31 August 1922) the *Guardian* newspaper concluded a long article by saying that 'Dr Rudolf Steiner's lectures, for which we express our very special thanks, brought to us in a very vivid way an ideal of humanity in education. He spoke to us about teachers who, freely and unitedly, unrestricted by external prescriptions and regimentation, develop their educational methods exclusively out of a thorough knowledge of human nature. He spoke to us about a kind of knowledge needed by the teacher, a knowledge of the being of man and the world, which is at the same time scientific and also penetrates into the most intimate inner life, which is intuitive and artistic.' It is a matter of concern to realize how we have strayed, in some of the ordinary teaching practices of today, from such educational ideals.

A year later, in 1923, it was through Margaret MacMillan, the indomitable pioneer of the nursery school movement, that Steiner came to give his cycle of 14 lectures in Ilkley, Derbyshire. It is published in book form as *A Modern Art of Education* and has been referred to as 'one of the most comprehensive introductions to his philosophy, psychology and practice of education'. Margaret MacMillan herself presided at its opening.

A second major course was given that year at Penmaenmawr, north Wales. The initiative for this originated with D.N. Dunlop, the well-known industrialist and a man of deep spiritual understanding. He had met Steiner only the year before and now asked him to speak 'out of the heart of anthroposophy'. Thus this course (*The Evolution of Consciousness*) as well as the one later published as *True and False Paths in Spiritual Investigation* given at a second Summer School organized by Dunlop (Torquay 1924) belong to the most fundamental expositions of modern spiritual development.

Between these two events a seminal conference took place at Dornach in Switzerland (Christmas 1923) at which Rudolf Steiner himself took on the leadership of the newly formed worldwide Anthroposophical Society, giving it at the same time a new esoteric foundation.

Conclusion

The last year of Steiner's life formed a climax of his activity. He began to speak in detail about the successive earth-lives of many historical personalities, always asking his audience to take these communications with the utmost tact, and warning against any form of sensationalism. He also held further courses for doctors, teachers, actors, eurythmists and theologians. He gave frequent talks, too, to the workmen at the Goetheanum and who often asked him to speak to them about the most varied aspects of life.

When Rudolf Steiner died, on 30 March 1925, he had, apart from any other activities, written 20 books and given more than 5000 lectures. He left altogether a remarkable achievement of work. What is equally important is the fact that many initiatives for new work in different fields have sprung from his ideas and from his encouragement of self-development. They continue to do so.

Walk On

As every flower must fade and all that's young
Must yield to age, so blossoms every step
In life all knowledge too but all that's good
Must have its time and pass perforce away.

With every summons to go on, the heart
Must say 'farewell', and then begin again,
Courageously, no mourning for the past,
Accept new patterns in the web of life.

In every new beginning there's a charm
Protecting us and helping us to live.
We are to walk from place to place serenely,
And not to cling to any one like home.
The spirit of the world does not constrain us
But wants to raise us upwards step by step.

Scarce are we settled in a realm of life
That slackness threatens us, it's only those
Who're ready to be up and on their way
That can escape from crippling habitudes.

Maybe e'en the hour of death will lead us on,
Renewed in spirit, to new territories,
The summons to go forward never ends ...
Take leave, my soul, and know that all is well.

Hermann Hesse (1877–1962)
Translation by Siegfried Rudel (with thanks to Richard Allen)

Further Reading

Rudolf Steiner, *The Course of My Life*, Anthroposophic Press, NY 1970

Rudolf Steiner, *Intuitive Thinking as a Spiritual Path—A Philosophy of Freedom*, Anthroposophic Press, NY 1995

Rudolf Steiner, *The Riddles of Philosophy*, Anthroposophic Press, NY 1973

Rudolf Steiner, *Christianity as Mystical Fact*, Anthroposophic Press, NY 1997

Rudolf Steiner, *Theosophy—An Introduction to the Spiritual Processes in Human Life and in the Cosmos*, Anthroposophic Press, NY 1994

Rudolf Steiner, *How to Know Higher Worlds—A Modern Path to Initiation*, Anthroposophic Press, NY 1994

Rudolf Steiner, *An Outline of Esoteric Science*, Anthroposophic Press, NY 1997

Rudolf Steiner, *Towards Social Renewal*, Rudolf Steiner Press, 1977

Rudolf Steiner, *Education for Special Needs—The Curative Education Course*, Rudolf Steiner Press, 1988

Rudolf Steiner, *Spiritual Foundations for a Renewal of Agriculture*, Bio-Dynamic Farming and Gardening Association, USA 1993

Rudolf Steiner, *Soul Economy and Waldorf Education*, Anthroposophic Press, NY 1986

Rudolf Steiner, *The Spiritual Ground of Education*, Anthroposophic Press, NY 2004

Rudolf Steiner, *A Modern Art of Education*, Rudolf Steiner Press, 1972

Rudolf Steiner, *True and False Paths in Spiritual Investigation*, Rudolf Steiner Press, 1985

E. Pfeiffer, *Soil Fertility, Renewal and Preservation*, Floris Books

E. Pfeiffer, *The Earth's Face—Landscape and the Health of the Soil*, Floris Books

Various Authors: *A Man Before Others—Rudolf Steiner Remembered*, Rudolf Steiner Press, 1993

T.H. Meyer, *D.N. Dunlop—A Man of Our Time*, Temple Lodge, 1992

A.P. Shepherd, *Rudolf Steiner—Scientist of the Invisible*, Floris Books, 1991

Frans Carlgren, *Education Towards Freedom*, Floris Books